Communica
with Children
When a Parent *is*
at the End of Life

of related interest

Children Also Grieve
Talking about Death and Healing
Linda Goldman
ISBN 978 1 84310 808 5
eISBN 978 1 84642 471 7

Talking with Children and Young People about Death and Dying
2nd edition
Mary Turner
Illustrated by Bob Thomas
ISBN 978 1 84310 441 4
eISBN 978 1 84642 560 8

Talking About Death and Bereavement in School
How to Help Children Aged 4 to 11 to Feel Supported and Understood
Ann Chadwick
ISBN 978 1 84905 246 7
eISBN 978 0 85700 527 4

Great Answers to Difficult Questions about Death
What Children Need to Know
Linda Goldman
ISBN 978 1 84905 805 6
eISBN 978 1 84642 957 6

Grief in Children
A Handbook for Adults
2nd edition
Atle Dyregrov
Foreword by Professor William Yule
ISBN 978 1 84310 612 8
eISBN 978 1 84642 781 7

Talking With Bereaved People
An Approach for Structured and Sensitive Communication
Dodie Graves
ISBN 978 1 84310 988 4
eISBN 978 0 85700 162 7

Overcoming Loss
Activities and Stories to Help Transform Children's Grief and Loss
Julia Sorensen
Illustrated by Maryam Ahmad
ISBN 978 1 84310 646 3
eISBN 978 1 84642 813 5

The Colors of Grief
Understanding a Child's Journey through Loss from Birth to Adulthood
Janis A. Di Ciacco
ISBN 978 1 84310 886 3
eISBN 978 1 84642 812 8

Communicating *with* Children *When a* Parent *is* *at the* End of Life

Rachel Fearnley

Jessica Kingsley *Publishers*
London and Philadelphia

First published in 2012
by Jessica Kingsley Publishers
116 Pentonville Road
London N1 9JB, UK
and
400 Market Street, Suite 400
Philadelphia, PA 19106, USA

www.jkp.com

Library of Congress Cataloging in Publication Data
Fearnley, Rachel, 1964-
  Communicating with children when a parent is at the end of life / Rachel Fearnley.
    p. cm.
  Includes bibliographical references and index.
  ISBN 978-1-84905-234-4 (alk. paper)
  1. Children of sick parents. 2. Sick--Family relationships. 3. Parents--Death--
Psychological aspects. 4. Interpersonal communication in children. I. Title.
  BF723.P25F43 2012
  155.9'37083--dc23
                            2011039024

British Library Cataloguing in Publication Data
A CIP catalogue record for this book is available from the British Library

ISBN 978 1 84905 234 4
eISBN 978 0 85700 475 8

Printed and bound in Great Britain

*To my parents who taught me
so much about life and death.*

Acknowledgements

I would like to thank my husband Barry for all his unreserved love, support and encouragement and for being my constant fellow traveller. Without his support and quiet belief in what I am doing, the writing of this book would have been a much lonelier, harder journey.

Chapters 5 and 6 have been co-written with Stephanie Barker, consultant nurse and systemic family therapist at Norfolk Community Health and Care Trust. She has over 28 years' experience of working in cancer and palliative care. I am indebted to Stephanie, whose contribution to the book has been invaluable. Stephanie's support and guidance have been really important, both in our professional relationship and as a friend. Her contribution to Chapters 5 and 6 has offered a dimension that otherwise would have been lacking and for this I am truly grateful.

I am very grateful too to Dr Carole Comben for reading early chapters and providing a critical eye just when I needed one, and for gently offering sound advice that has been invaluable. I would also like to thank Caroline Walton of Jessica Kingsley Publishers for all her help and support.

Finally, I must acknowledge all the children who have inspired the writing of this book. I sincerely hope that I have honoured their voices and in some small way helped to promote the need for timely, open and honest communication about parental dying and death.

Contents

Preface

As a young nursery nurse, I always loved the prospect of story time with the children. It was scheduled for the end of the session and was a quiet, relaxing time. It gave me the opportunity to enter the children's worlds with stories of fantasy, exploration and imagination. I was able to show my creative side and my love of books allowed me to share something very special with the children. I had many favourite stories but one that I always particularly enjoyed reading was *Not Now Bernard* (McKee 1980). It had a simple text and bright pictures but most of all I could become totally expressive as I read the story. For people unfamiliar with the plot, Bernard is a young boy who tries in vain to talk to his parents, including telling them about a monster that is lurking in the garden. Sadly, they are too busy doing important tasks around the home. Bernard retreats to the garden where he is eaten by the monster. The monster then goes into the house and tries in his own way to communicate with Bernard's parents. They ignore him, despite his monster-like ways to communicate with them. Eventually, Bernard's mother sends him to bed with a milky drink. The monster protests his identity but 'Bernard' is still ignored by the mother and the final pictures are of the monster in Bernard's bed and Bernard's mother turning off the bedroom light as she retreats onto the landing.

Today I am reminded of the book; with a little wisdom between me, the young nursery nurse and the now older academic, the salience of the text is still very prevalent. The protagonist, Bernard, has important information that he desperately wants to impart to his parents. However, both parents are too busy, too caught up in their adult worlds, adult jobs and adult problems to hear him and to take time to listen to him.

The current book is written about a specific group of children whose lives are at risk of sharing many parallels with Bernard's. These are children who are living with a parent who is at the end of life. These children, too, are frequently not listened to or included in conversations about what is happening within their families, and they are at risk of becoming marginalised. I will argue that, when children are living within the volatile world of parental terminal illness, their needs are often diluted in favour of the medical needs of their ill parent. The adults in the children's lives are like Bernard's parents – they are too busy and too entrenched in their adult worlds and adult problems to recognise the importance of communication, information sharing and listening.

This book is written for professionals working in health, social care and education who are likely to come into contact with children whose parents are terminally ill. Some practitioners are more likely to work with this population of children than others – for example, nurses who specialise in palliative care or nurse people with life-threatening illness, social workers and teachers – while others may not routinely meet children who are living with a parent who is dying, but might do under specific circumstances. The idea for the book was borne from two converging experiences – first, my years of practice in social care and, more recently, my doctoral research. My research explored children's experiences when living with a parent who is dying. Participants included parents, professionals working in health and social care and, importantly, children who had been bereaved of a parent. This was a qualitative study where the emphasis was on people's stories about their experiences and observations. The key finding to emerge from the research was the importance children placed on communication and information sharing during this period. All the accounts that I was privileged to hear returned again and again to the importance of communication. It therefore feels appropriate that the story of my hero Bernard can teach us all so much about communication and children, and particularly children who are living with a parent who is dying.

Chapter 1

Why Communication?

Childhood is recognised as a time of growth, development and change. Children's lives are typically punctuated with changes and challenges, some of which are ubiquitous and generally seen as rites of passage. Others are less common and have the ability to destabilise life and to rock the very core of the children. Living with a parent who is dying is an example of such:

> We in the western world live with a paradox: death is all around us, yet we believe that if we do not talk with children about death, it will not touch them. We try to protect and insulate them from this fact of life, which is typically associated with anxiety and pain. (Silverman 2000, p.2)

Silverman's quote was written over a decade ago; yet the paradox remains and some would argue that it has become ever more entrenched. Despite advancements in many aspects of our lives during the last decade, the positioning of children in relation to dying and death appears to have stagnated. Typically, children continue to be shielded from this reality in their lives and as a result are silenced and rendered invisible. Whether it is because of genuine concern to protect, misguided views of children's capacity to cope or a sense that they do not need to be included, it is time that positive action is taken to give these children a voice and for their situation to be truly recognised and acknowledged by the '3 P's': policy makers, professionals and parents. Professionals, especially those working directly with terminally ill people, have a role in cascading this recognition to parents, and, equally, policy makers have a duty to influence practice and have the courage to put such an important issue on the agenda.

The focus of the book is firmly rooted in the 'middle P's': the professionals working with terminally ill patients and their families. A theme throughout will be that professionals have a role in unlocking the silence and encouraging the facilitation of communication so that children are involved in the family crisis that is unfolding and can, with support, begin to make meaning from what is happening. By mirroring good practice, this can then be extended to parents, while also helping to shape and embed future policies that recognise this population of children.

Living with a dying parent is a unique experience for children and there is no one formula that can be assigned. To this extent, it is likely that siblings living in the same household, and who are thrown into the same situation, will experience it differently. Character, personality and the relationship with the parent are aspects that will influence how children experience what is occurring. However, the overarching factors fundamental to children living with a parent who is dying are communication, information sharing and involvement. This book will explore the relevance of communication and information sharing, and will provide practical examples for developing confidence and competence when working with such children.

Throughout the book, the metaphor of a journey is used to describe and illustrate children's experiences of living with a terminally ill parent. The representation of a journey is symbolic in exploring the children's lives through the lens of a researcher practitioner.

Although in my life I have shared some parts of a similar journey, I also need to acknowledge that each journey is unique and will begin and end at different points along the way. Some journeys will be short in duration, especially when the imminent death is due to trauma or the nature of the illness makes it so. Other journeys will be longer and involve many twists and turns. These long journeys occasionally travel through hope but rarely do they end anywhere other than in sadness and grief. When children are accompanied on this journey with trusted family, friends and professionals, it can be a less traumatic excursion into the unknown. When you are the driver, you have more control regarding the route, stopping-off points and how you reach the destination. When you are the passenger, the choices are fewer; children are usually the passengers in their own journey, with limited choice. Professionals are in a privileged position because they can enable children to take control of the wheel for at least some of their journey.

This book is written for professionals who in the course of their working lives will work with children who are living with a parent who is dying. For some professionals, these are regular encounters – for example, nurses, doctors and specialist social workers are particularly likely to work with families where a parent has a terminal diagnosis, as on occasions are funeral directors. Other professionals – for example, teachers, family support workers and youth workers – may not expect, in the day-to-day course of their work, to find themselves needing to support this potentially vulnerable population of children; however, statistically, during their careers, they will meet children whose parents are dying. Throughout the book, I will refer to professionals and practitioners interchangeably and generically. However, when I am referring to a specific profession, I will note this.

In harmony with my strongly held belief that clearer and more accessible language should be used when communicating with children, the writing of the book will adopt a similar standpoint. It will therefore embrace a conversational tone that I sincerely hope will reflect the importance of communication and language when working with children and their families.

Underpinning the book are the concepts of communication and information sharing, and there will be an exploration throughout of how these two interrelated aspects are of imperative significance for children when they are living with a parent who is dying. The term 'information' is used here specifically to describe the knowledge that children gain about their parent's illness. It includes both factual knowledge about prognosis, extent, severity and stage of the illness, and emotional knowledge about feelings, fears and hopes for the future. The term 'communication' is used specifically to describe *how* children come by this information.

I suggest that children frequently move into what I term an 'alien landscape' when living with parents who are in the terminal stages of their illnesses. I use the metaphor of an alien landscape to try to capture the impression that many children feel a sense of disorientation arising from the loss of much that was previously known and familiar. The children's view of their world takes on new and difficult meanings, and any control or autonomy they feel they previously enjoyed is frequently lost or diluted. Family routines are interrupted and the ill parent's illness and treatment become the nucleus of family life. Furthermore, some of the different cultures that make up the children's world can be affected and become increasingly uncomfortable and contradictory.

During parental terminal illness, the culture of the family is often the primary example of a location where children feel that they are living in an unpredictable and unfamiliar place. Patterns of communication frequently alter along with the parent's established parenting style. These changes contribute to the children feeling that their known worlds are becoming disrupted and different. Once the familiar boundaries and routines are lost, the children's sense of who they are and what their family represents is questioned and, as a consequence, has the potential to turn what once felt familiar and safe into an increasingly frightening and alien landscape.

The rich diversity of modern family life needs to be recognised and acknowledged. The traditional nuclear family where stereotypical roles were assigned to family members has become, generally, a thing of history books and nostalgic television programmes. In modern, cosmopolitan Britain, there is no longer one 'family' type, and children are growing up in eclectic situations that previous generations would have baulked at. Children experience diversity in family life that should be celebrated and nurtured. My simplified usage of the term 'family' is therefore not used in a disparaging manner, but rather for brevity. Moreover, it would be disrespectful to the children to cluster their experiences into one homogeneous group. No matter what their family circumstances are, children living with a parent who is dying will face a unique set of experiences that are personal and relevant to them. The composition of their family and how it functions may have a part to play in how they manage the situation; however, other factors will also have a role.

For the purpose of the book, I have adopted the Children Act 1989 definition of children and have therefore included all children, up to their 18th birthday, who are experiencing the death of a parent. Therefore, for succinctness within the text, I will write generically about children (rather than using the phrase 'children and young people') unless I am specifically describing adolescents' and older children's experiences. In these instances I will refer to them as 'young people'. Furthermore, in relation to the adopted discourse throughout the book, when I use the umbrella term 'service user' to describe people who access services, this will include patients and clients.

The focus of the book and the majority of references are made to terminal illness where people are aware that a parent has a life-limiting illness or disease that will shorten their life. Some children will live for many years with an awareness that their parent is ill, before the illness becomes terminal. For these children, the culture of illness becomes part of their normative experience. However, it needs to be acknowledged that death as a result of serious trauma, accident or sudden onset of illness will also be a feature of some children's lives. In these circumstances, the period between the incident and death could be very short and opportunities for preparing or supporting the children limited. In these situations, though, they are still catapulted into an alien landscape but their journey is often swift and there is little time to note any significant markers that might provide some indication of their terrain.

The extent of a professional's involvement with the children may be very limited, even when the parent is known to the medical establishment and there is some time between the terminal diagnosis and death. However, the value of their work cannot be underestimated. Appropriate interventions and support can be the difference between a relatively straightforward journey and a complicated one. I am not suggesting that the intervention from a professional is a panacea and that through this the children will not encounter any difficulties. However, with appropriate support, especially in the form of communication and information sharing, the children will be offered better opportunities to discover their own resources for coping with the inevitable challenges that they will face. An important factor is that what and how we communicate can have a lasting effect on how children cope and manage a situation both in the short and longer term. Professionals need to be cognisant that their involvement with children may be limited but nevertheless very intense. Therefore, what is important is how the working relationship develops and, essentially, how its ending is planned. For the children, amid all the other changes that are occurring, the termination of the work could have negative consequences in reflecting a current life experience that is already peppered with loss.

Bereaved children have been termed 'the forgotten mourners' (Smith 1999) and Doka (1989) introduced the notion of disenfranchised grief, whereby children are often not recognised as mourners. However, I argue that while this is all too often the case, children who are living with a dying parent are equally, if not at times *more*, excluded and rendered silent by society. These children are rarely recognised by policies at the local or national level. For example, in the Government's

Green Paper *Every Child Matters* (Department for Education and Skills 2003), this population of children is not mentioned, which begs the question, 'Does every child really matter?' (Willis 2005). Moreover, few schools within the United Kingdom have in place policies for working with dying and death. Some years ago when I was a school governor, I asked why we had a policy for bomb scares (which were rare in the small northern town) and nothing for dying and death. I received a sharp taking in of air from a colleague and a look of utter horror from the headteacher! Within academic literature, these children receive scant attention when compared with the needs of other minority groups and service provision is, on the whole, pitiful. However, within the *Every Child Matters* literature there is a drive for change in how children's services are delivered, including:

- improved outcomes for children to ensure that they are healthy, stay safe, enjoy and achieve, make a positive contribution and achieve economic well-being

- support for parents, carers and families, and

- a shift to preventation, early identification and intervention.

(Hunt 2006, p.39)

A significant element to the Children Act 2004 is the improvement of children's lives through improved provision, including universal services and more targeted services for children who have additional needs. However, despite now being enshrined in law for over six years, there appears to be limited filtration into services for children whose parents are dying. This is despite the fact that they are less likely to meet the five outcomes of *Every Child Matters* and are therefore more at risk than their peers who are living with healthy parents. Here it is important to stress that I am not suggesting that all children whose parents are terminally ill are at risk, as defined by the Children Act 1989; however, I am suggesting that as a group they are at increased risk because of their current lived experience. Furthermore, I believe that it is imperative that professionals recognise this and offer appropriate and timely support to such families to prevent potential difficulties.

Transitions, changes and challenges associated with living with a parent who is dying

Children who are living with a parent who is dying face many transitions, changes and challenges. The childhood years are typically marked by a progression of transitions or key turning points through which children grow and develop a sense of identity, belonging and family membership. This may not always be a positive experience; adolescence, for example, is characteristically marked by crises of self-confidence, uncertainty and ambivalence. However, when a parent is at the end of life, children are likely to experience many transitions that are unique and specific to their current circumstances. These changes affect children irrespective of their age, gender or previous relationship with the parent. The children move from living within a safe boundaried world, within their current situated living environment, to experiencing uncertainty, chaos and confusion, and they are forced to enter a world where their taken-for-granted lives are lost.

Within the myriad of difficult and painful challenges that children are forced to contemplate when a parent is diagnosed with a terminal illness, perhaps the hardest one to cope with is the shift from having a healthy parent to knowing that the parent is ill and is going to die. Within this awareness, children are forced to cope with a number of different transitions psychologically, cognitively and socially. Each of these can create changes and challenges (Way 2009) at the individual level but also within the construct of the family and the wider social community. Knowing that a parent is going to die, and anticipating the changing future, force the children into a liminal period where their known life is suspended. With the knowledge that the ill parent is going to die, all that was safe and predictable within their world is shattered and potentially lost for ever. The children are thrown into an alien landscape where all previously known rules, contours and maps have been reluctantly discarded and replaced with a poorly defined map that offers little reassurance to the traveller of their position or possible route through. Critical turning points occur throughout the illness trajectory; however, these are often unpredictable and cannot be planned for with any certainty. As a consequence, the children are compelled to pass through this period with little control.

Within this alien landscape uncertainty is a constant companion and one which, without careful management, will play any number of tricks on the children in an attempt to confuse and frighten them. However, uncertainty can be reined in and put in its rightful place if appropriate support is offered to the children. The most important and effective form of support, the one that uncertainty fears the most, is communication and information sharing. With the appropriate levels of communication and information sharing being made available on a consistent basis, the challenges that the children face can be, if not minimised, drastically reduced.

Children becoming invisible

A major challenge that such children experience is their in effect becoming invisible as a result of not being included in any conversations about their parent's illness. As a result of this prohibitive behaviour, they are silenced and do not have a voice. It is easy to understand how the enormity of the bombshell of a terminal diagnosis can cause parents to go into emotional free fall. Even if they have been ill for some time and have lived with the knowledge that the illness might become terminal, the actual process of receiving the news is utterly devastating. Their hopes, dreams and aspirations are lost in one short interview with a doctor. As the weight of the bombshell begins to sink in, they may feel a natural instinctive desire to protect their children. An element of this protective behaviour is often played out by excluding children from any conversations or information sharing about the illness and its likely trajectory. However, this behaviour is, more often than not, a false economy because it actually exposes children to more uncertainty and fear. I will argue throughout this book that children will know that a crisis is unfolding within their family and, without adequate involvement, they will be at risk of exclusion at a time when they need to be included.

When children, no matter their age, are ignored, they are being given a clear message that they are not sufficiently responsible or mature to be included in something major that is occurring within their family. Being excluded at a time of great change only serves to increase their anxiety. Not knowing is almost always worse than knowing; after all, if they are in receipt of factual information about their parent's illness, they can then make informed choices about the extent of their involvement. Furthermore, they are not left feeling that they have been excluded because the impending crisis is so horrific that they need to be protected from it. This is borne out by Silverman who attests that 'stress for a child may come from adults not recognizing them as mourners and failing to include them in the family drama' (2000, p.26).

How many stories abound of children being sent away to stay with family members, only to return some time later and then be informed that their parent has 'gone away'? These stories, which transcend generations, affect children not only at the time of their exclusion but generally throughout their lives. Not telling children about their parent's illness might appear not to have the same magnitude as removing them to a relative's house; nevertheless, the implications are consistent. Being excluded when the family is experiencing major upheaval and a life-changing crisis can create a deep and permanent scar on the children's emotional and psychological biography. The lack of involvement can result in prolonged sadness, difficulties adjusting to life without the parent, and unresolved grief. When I was in practice, many of the families that were referred to the service for support came because of unresolved grief. For many of these adult service users, their grief had remained locked away deep in their unconscious mind, only to surface when they had their own family. The silencing and resultant exclusion from their parent's death, often some 10 or 15 years previously, created untold trauma that returned to haunt them when they themselves became parents.

Encouraging parents to involve their children in conversations and information sharing about the illness enables the children to have a voice and to become visible. Relinquishing the silence in favour of inclusion helps them to participate in something that will be having a huge impact on all aspects of their lives. Moreover, as this inclusion develops, an inverse correlation takes place: the more they are included, the more their fears are likely to subside. Within the alien landscape that they have entered, they move from being in a place that offers few clues as to their whereabouts to a position of knowing something about their location. The contours of the landscape become clearer the more they are included and with this comes a feeling of some control.

The impact of the parent's care on the children – further challenges and changes

The general confusion and upheaval that children experience, when in this major transitional period of moving from living with a parent who is well to living with one who is dying, is exacerbated by the parent's medical treatment and whether this is provided at home, in hospital or in a hospice. My research highlighted how the parent's increasing dependence on nursing care can cause a major challenge for children and leave them questioning their identity and belonging within the family.

The hospital or hospice environment

When the parent is hospitalised, the children need to make adjustments to their daily routines and, importantly, how they see the world. Spontaneity in relation to seeing the parent is lost in an instant and the children become reliant on others to facilitate visits to the hospital. The admission to hospital or a hospice means that visiting times are generally prescribed and need to be planned and prepared for. Consequently, the spontaneity of conversations and general chit-chat is lost and needs to be managed within the allotted visiting time. For participants in my research, some of the issues related to not being able to have some connectedness with the parent. Opportunities for shared time together are lost. Taken-for-granted activities that act as the glue of family life become more difficult to manage. For example, reading a book together becomes increasingly problematic, partly because of the parent's deteriorating health but also because of the clinical environment where the children and the parents meet. Therefore, for the children there are difficult, unanswered questions about why their familiar and predictable routines are lost. Questions about intent are likely to surface – for example, 'Has Mummy stopped loving me and is that why she won't read to me any more?' Younger children are particularly likely to make the misconnection and draw erroneous conclusions about the situation. It is therefore vital that children are provided with an ongoing dialogue about what is happening and why. Nursing and medical staff have a substantial role here in facilitating such conversations and including the children so that they are equipped with the relevant knowledge to allow them to make some meaning from what is happening.

The hospital or hospice environment rarely lends itself to privacy and, as a consequence, a further opportunity for spontaneity is lost. Children are expected to behave in a prescribed way; they have to be quiet and respectful because of the other patients, and they are very much constrained. However, while adults generally have a 'script' to work to when visiting someone in hospital, children more often than not do not have an appropriate script to hand. Younger children in particular struggle to understand why they cannot sit on the bed with their parent or charge round the ward as they would at home. It is therefore important to explain to them what it will be like when they visit their parent. This information should include the sights and smells they are likely to encounter and they should be given some explanation about the machines and equipment that will be visible. This is particularly true for children visiting parents in High Dependency Units (HDUs) and Intensive Treatment Units (ITUs). If the patient is on a ventilator and has numerous tubes and wires attached, this can be an alarming sight for adults, let alone children. These specialist units, with their cacophony of bleeps and monitors, present particular challenges to children and additional support may be required. The personnel on these wards need to be especially vigilant if children are going to be visiting so that they can be well prepared for what they are going to see. These issues are discussed again in Chapter 6.

It is important to recognise that children will be faced with many new experiences when visiting a very ill parent and these just compound the feelings of entry into an alien landscape. Moreover, the realisation for children, of whatever age, that their parent is in hospital or a hospice will often be the stimulus for recognition of the serious nature of the illness. Being faced with the enormity of the changes in family life when the parent is hospitalised can often be the trigger for children to realise how ill their parent is. If parents are being cared for in a hospice, it is highly probable that during their admission other patients will die. This close to hand awareness of death has the potential to send powerful messages to children about the setting in which their parents are being cared for. When death is part of the culture of the environment, children need to have age-appropriate explanations given about what is likely to happen there. It is therefore imperative that children are recognised as key people within the life of the hospice who need to be included, not excluded. Moreover, in these situations, the hospice needs to have robust procedures in place to facilitate the management of death so that those who are witnessing the events can be sensitively and appropriately supported.

Visiting the parent in hospital or the hospice: a matter of choice

It is important that the parents consider the children's needs when planning hospital or hospice visits. Professionals can help in this by encouraging them to think about giving the children choice. Although the natural assumption is that they will want to visit their parent, for some children this is not the case. The false and often scary environment, along with the enforced strained opportunities for spontaneous interaction, often mean that children would prefer not to visit their parent in hospital or a hospice. When this reluctance is seen through the eyes of the child, it can be more easily understood. Such environments represent illness, pain and suffering. Some children may equate these feelings to their own experiences of hospital life when they have been ill, while for others the strong emotions are anchored securely in the here and now. The emotional pain of seeing parents in such a location is difficult to comprehend and can create memories that then compete with happier memories of the parents when they were at home. Moreover, the illness and its treatment may bring about changes in their personality. These changes can be frightening to children and cause confusion and more uncertainty. If the changes are not explained to them sensitively, they may wrongly assume that this change in behaviour is a result of something they have done or because the parent does not love them any more. These misinterpretations of the situation could be a reason why children do not want to visit the hospital or hospice. After all, if the changes are as a result of something you have done, or, even worse, because your mummy or daddy has stopped loving you, the best course of action is to avoid the situation.

The well parent who is understandably wrapped up in the emotionally strained situation may feel that the children have to visit the hospital on every occasion and that, if they do not, they are demonstrating some form of disrespect to the ill parent. Helping both parents to understand that children may find the experience too painful, frightening or difficult to comprehend may offer them a better understanding of what their children are probably feeling and thinking. However, practical arrangements need to be considered: if the well parent is visiting the hospital or hospice without the children, child care needs to be arranged. Professionals involved with the family can pre-empt this by exploring with the parent the use of appropriate, reliable and safe baby-sitters.

Challenges when the parent is cared for at home

When the parent is being nursed in hospital or a hospice, children face a number of challenges that shake their known world. However, there are also changes and transitions presented when the parent is being cared for at home. Having regular home visits from the medical team creates changes and challenges from 'normal' family life into a very different home life. One young person in my research observed that, when the nurses and doctors started coming to the house, this was when they realised how serious it all was. When someone is being nursed at home, this necessitates much concentrated physical care. Typically the presentation of the house is altered; suddenly lots of different equipment is brought into the house and it takes on a new personality. With this comes what is often seen as an endless parade of people visiting the house including nurses, doctors and specialist support staff. Each of these professionals has a different task to perform and invariably this is in relation to the patient's care, not the emotional well-being of the children. Having so many different people around can create instability and fear in the children. Not knowing why all these people are coming to the house, or their role and function, can be alarming and confusing and add to the feelings of isolation. Moreover, with the constant stream of people entering the home, all control is removed from the family and placed within the professionals' domain, thus highlighting to the children their limited power or control of the situation.

The loss of spontaneity was discussed in relation to children visiting their parent in hospital; however, this might also be the situation when the parent is being nursed at home. Moments of privacy and intimacy are disrupted because of the nursing and medical care, and suddenly everything is on show to all the strangers who are coming into the home.

The family home becomes a micro-hospital, which results in dramatic changes to how it is perceived. Whatever 'home' meant to the children before illness became part of family life is likely to be disrupted and challenged. The main room where the family used to congregate and relax may have become the patient's bedroom and, as a result, a further marker for identity loss. The constant comings and goings of different people, all of who are focused on the ill parent, means that the children are forced to redefine their lives. Moreover, this redefining needs to happen quickly to accommodate all the changes. It therefore represents an upheaval that requires careful management to help maintain some normality and provide the children with a reference point.

Cohesion of group identity

A challenge that many children experience, having entered the alien landscape of parental terminal illness, is the ability to maintain relationships with peers. The reality of living with a parent who is dying is that children take on new and unwelcome identities. Their preferred identity is snatched away from them as they are thrown into the turbulent world of illness and death. Children do not generally like to be different from their peers; group identity and cohesion are important in being 'one of the crowd' and in helping to form their biography. Participants in my research described how children will go to great lengths to hide, from friends, the news that their parent is dying. They are in effect attempting to shield themselves so that they can remain 'the same' as friends.

I believe that a significant factor in this protective behaviour is the fear of not being able to talk to friends about what is happening. Friends are often great confidants but, if they do not understand the contours of the map and cannot therefore begin to appreciate what the landscape looks like, they are not in a position to empathise. Children become different because of the nature of their current experience and a factor in this perceived difference is the general taboo that society has about dying and death. There is a significant taboo about talking about death; therefore, children whose parents are dying struggle to talk to their friends and their friends, in turn, struggle to know what to say to them. This in itself creates a chasm that, once open, is difficult to bridge. Children's knowledge and understanding of death is often stilted and comes from erroneous sources, especially the media where death is often sensationalised. Therefore, friends who have limited experience are unable to engage in meaningful conversations that could help in defining the child within the group. Children involved in my research talked about feigning an identity to appear the same as friends, and 'putting on a smile' and pretending that they were okay because friends did not understand. These feelings of difference can be overwhelming and are yet further indicators to the children that they are living in the midst of changes that affect every aspect of their lives.

The social life of the children

Home life, as the children know it, alters and the predictability of life that is so reassuringly mundane is thrown into upheaval. The illness becomes the nucleus of family life with all conversations and actions being based on the care of the patient. This upheaval inexorably spills over into the children's social lives and inadvertently creates alienation and marginalisation from the social world, and more specifically the social activities that they had enjoyed and participated in prior to the parent becoming ill.

Time constraints placed on the family, whether due to hospital visiting or the medical regime within the home, are a significant barrier preventing children from engaging in the activities they previously enjoyed. Moreover, the financial cost of attendance could also have implications for children, particularly when one or both of the household incomes are depleted or lost because of the illness. Not being able to participate as before, for whatever reason, is likely to add to the children's feelings of isolation and being different. Children generally do not like to feel different: it is important to them to belong in their peer group and to 'fit in'. When their participation in social activities is curtailed because of the parent's illness, they are at risk of becoming disconnected from friends who act as identity beacons in their lives.

Changes in parental capacity

The upheaval of parental terminal illness brings with it subsidiary difficulties. A major challenge within these changes is how parents continue to parent their children and parents often experience a diminishing sense of parenting efficacy (Saldinger *et al.* 2004a). In these circumstances it is often the situation that the boundaries and routines, set by the parents and previously in force, dissipate under the pressure of coping emotionally and physically with the situation. Children thrive on having regular routines and boundaries. These are important for ensuring that they feel safe and, although throughout childhood children will test boundaries to the limit, they are vital in forming a sense of security (Saldinger, Porterfield and Cain 2004b). When parents are diagnosed as being terminally ill, and the enormity of what they have to face becomes a reality, the importance of maintaining previously known boundaries is sometimes lost in the midst of the crisis. Occasionally these changes are a result of the parents being so embroiled in the situation that the children's needs become less paramount (Kennedy *et al.* 2008). A crisis of confidence in everything that was previously known can occur and as a consequence the parents, who prior to the illness were confident in their role, lose this confidence and feel that they are floundering in a sea of uncertainty. In other circumstances, parents deliberately alter their parenting style and the boundaries become blurred. This loosening of parental boundaries is often done in an effort to buffer the children from all that is happening. Parents believe that because the situation is so dire they should compensate for this by becoming more lenient with their children. Conversely of course, the opposite can also occur and parenting can become more rigid and controlled.

However, whatever the reason for this change in parenting styles, it typically only serves to add to the confusion that the children are increasingly feeling. The sudden lifting of the known boundaries, while being most children's dream scenario, can, in reality, have the effect of unsettling them and giving them a strong message that everything must be so awful that suddenly all parental control has gone. The changes that occur when this happens create bewilderment. Although the children probably struggle to understand why the changes have occurred, it is a further example to them of the apparent destabilising of their family life. When the previously known secure boundaries become blurred and less well defined, opportunities to test the extent of them are presented to the children. The initial loosening of boundaries may result in children feeling emancipated and they may take advantage of their new freedom. However, this freedom can also cause them to feel uncertain – after all, the familiar structures are crumbling around them and this can invoke insecurity. Therefore, children can be left in a condtradictory position: on one hand they suddenly have the freedom they have always dreamt about, but conversely they are missing the guidance that steers them through their lives. When these feelings are coupled with the uncertainty of the current crisis, children are faced with a complex series of changes and challenges.

The professional's role in supporting parenting

Professionals have a role here in working with parents to consider how their parenting is affecting the children. Providing the parents with strategies for helping to maintain their dominant style of parenting, while also offering reassurance about their capabilities, can be helpful. Encouraging them to think about how they previously parented their children, and to look at their earlier strengths, might be the small intervention required to help them restore boundaries for the children. Moreover, some preventative work with well parents, which explores how they will take on the role of single parent following the death, may also be of benefit. It is probable that the well parents have either not contemplated life following the death or are too emotionally preoccupied to consider their role once their partner has died. While such prospects are very painful to consider, the reality is that once the ill parent has died the children will still need to be cared for; however, they are also likely to have heightened needs because of the life-changing experience of parental death.

In some circumstances, surviving parents are so overwhelmed by their own grief that they are not in a position to recognise the needs of their children (Beale, Sivesind and Bruera 2004; Melvin and Lukeman 2000). Therefore, again the role of professionals is vitally important in supporting parents to contemplate their own emotional pain while thinking about the needs of their children. If some of these conversations are held before the death, they can offer a preventative precursor to the potential disruptions in parenting following the death. In this sense, the parents are being pre-warned of situations they might face, while at the same time being encouraged to begin to contemplate the future in the role of a single parent.

Charting the landscape of this book

The ideas from the book are drawn from practice, experience and research, and the importance of being proactive with families from, whenever possible, the early stages of the illness journey is advocated throughout. Having the opportunity to work with the children over time and thus being able to offer them information in small chunks is the preferred way of working and will help them to begin making some meaning from the situation. This approach also means that children are not bombarded with large amounts of information at the point when their parent's health has deteriorated to the extent that death is imminent. However, neither is the approach being advocated whereby they are given too much information too soon. Giving them incremental information about their parent's health is optimum. So therefore, when parents first receive the news that they have an illness that could become terminal, the headline news offered to the children should be that their parents are ill but there is treatment available to help them. If treatment stops being a viable option and care becomes palliative not curative, the children need to be given this news gently. However, if they have been included throughout the journey, this news, while being devastating, will not be such a huge shock.

Parents who are exposed to the news that the illness is terminal are forced to, very quickly, reconsider all aspects of their lives. Their hopes, dreams and plans for the future are shattered in one blow and somewhere within the midst of this crisis is the contemplation of what to do about the children. Is it better to protect them from what is happening or inform them at the risk of causing great upset? Telling children that one of their parents is dying must be one of the most difficult tasks (MacPherson 2005) and therefore the role of professionals is important here in supporting parents to begin thinking about how such a difficult task could be undertaken. MacPherson (2005) suggests that it is crucial that palliative care services offer specialised advice and support to couples to help them talk to their children about the illness and prognosis. However, within this book I will extend this proposal to argue that all professionals, whether in specialist teams or not, have a significant role in supporting these conversations.

The value of children being included in conversations about their parent's illness and prognosis has been documented (Christ 2000a; Christ and Christ 2006; Rauch, Muriel and Cassem 2002; Thastum *et al.* 2008) and this theme underpins the book, with particular emphasis on the contribution practitioners can make in this process. Siegel, Mesagno and Christ (1990) write about the importance of open parent–child communication, when a parent is terminally ill, in helping children resolve painful feelings and correct their distorted fantasies about what is occurring. However, when parents have to contemplate such difficult conversations, they often, not unreasonably, struggle with them. This is where the practitioners involved with the family have a significant role. They can support the parents, in the first instance, to recognise the value of such conversations and, second, to think about the content of the conversations. Throughout the book the value, for the children, of being included will be emphasised. No matter how well parents try to conceal the illness from their children, the children will inevitably guess that something is wrong. By being included, they are able to begin to make sense of the situation and this meaning-making process will be based on fact rather than supposition. Moreover, when children are included, they are then permitted to have the opportunity to express their thoughts, feelings and worries more openly. This in turn alleviates feelings of isolation and exclusion from such a significant occurrence within their family.

Parents are generally best situated to have these conversations with their children; they know their children and also the communication culture in which they live. So the practitioner's role is often that of facilitator to help the parents begin to engage in dialogue with their children. However, there are also occasions when practitioners take on a more direct role and work specifically with the children, whether this be individually or with siblings or in conjunction with the parents. Both circumstances are explored in the book and professional discretion is called upon when assessing whether the work is best undertaken directly with the children or through supporting their parents.

It is not unlikely that during the course of working with families practitioners will meet with parents who voice strong opinions about not including the children in discussions about the illness. Under these circumstances, there is a fine balance to be drawn between respecting the parents' views and opinions and recognising the best interests of the children. Here it is advisable to explore with the parents their misgivings and to offer them an argument about the importance of children being included.

Although the focus of the book is rooted firmly in parents with terminal illness, it is important also to consider that the scenarios could easily equate to grandparents who are terminally ill. Grandparents often have a significant role in the care of their grandchildren and develop very special relationships. One young person in my research was very candid in describing how the grandparent was 'the most special person in my life'. It is therefore important, and good practice, to consider the needs of grandchildren and include them too in discussions.

The journey of the book begins with an exploration of what communication is. In Chapter 2 a discussion is presented about types of communication and how the use of appropriate language is so important in helping children create some sense of meaning about what is happening in their family. Different types of communication are discussed and how these relate to this population of children. The importance of language usage is discussed in this chapter and especially the harmful effect of euphemisms. Although euphemistic language is often used to 'protect' the receiver from the harsh reality of what is occurring, in truth it only serves to create confusion, especially in children whose cognitive and language skills are in a state of development. The use of euphemisms can contribute to the misunderstandings children make about what is happening (Waskett 1995) but they can also help to 'remove' the dead from normal life, thus enabling the living to continue with their lives (Riches and Dawson 2000). Throughout the chapter the relevance of the types of communication is referred to and explored through the practitioners' lens. This early explorative chapter also looks at child development and how children's understanding will typically be affected by their age and stage of development. This will again begin to offer practitioners a framework for revising knowledge and reflecting on their communication skills.

Chapter 3 considers how children begin to, or are inhibited from, making sense from what is happening. Much of this process can again be attributed to language, information sharing and the extent to which children are involved in conversations about their parent's illness. The chapter includes vignettes that illustrate how communication can act as a barrier to helping children begin to make some sense from the situation. There is an exploration of some of the barriers that are erected by parents when considering communicating with their children about what is happening within the family. Some barriers are used to deflect the pain away from children and to protect them from all that is happening, while others are employed in the belief that they are too young to understand or do not need to know. However, parents are not the only adults in children's lives who sometimes create barriers to communication and information sharing. Professionals working with a family will at times not only avoid talking to the children about what is happening but also consciously circumvent talking to the parents about including their children in the situation. This can result in lost opportunities to develop dialogue that would serve to help the children feel included in a situation that has the potential to paralyse them emotionally and socially when they are excluded. The final part of this chapter is dedicated to looking at practical ways that professionals can develop their confidence and competence in communicating with this population of children. Practical examples and vignettes are presented for practitioners to work through to help them feel more at ease when contemplating communicating with these children.

Chapter 4 presents the practical concept of the communication continuum. This continuum has been developed following my doctoral research and provides a practical application to a model when thinking about the extent of children's involvement in the communication and information-sharing process. The chapter begins with an outline of the concept and how it can be applied in practice. This is followed by an exploration of factors that help or hinder children's movement along the continuum and their positioning on it. The focus then moves to how professionals can utilise the continuum in their practice.

Chapter 5 is a practically orientated chapter and I am delighted that this, along with Chapter 6, has been co-written with Stephanie Barker. Stephanie is a highly experienced consultant nurse, whom I have been privileged to know for a number of years. Her contribution to the writing of the book has been invaluable and has offered a dimension that otherwise would have been lacking. Within Chapter 5, we begin by thinking about communication from the children's perspective and how important it is for them to be listened to. The need for them to have a voice, and through this to develop a more robust narrative about their current life experience, is explored along with consideration of how children can be helped to find their voice. The focus then moves towards the practicalities of working with children and their families in these particular circumstances. This includes an exploration of general rules for talking to children, including issues of confidentiality and roles and responsibilities. The chapter then looks at resources available to practitioners to help facilitate conversations with children. Finally, the chapter considers specific professions and their particular roles in helping children to communicate.

The content of Chapter 6 is slightly different from that of earlier chapters in that we consider not only expected deaths but also sudden deaths and how professionals can support children in these different circumstances. The chapter again begins by considering issues relating to anticipated deaths but then moves on to discuss sudden deaths. First, this is in relation to the ITU and working with children, including consideration of the environment and the process of helping them say goodbye to their parent. The focus then moves to sudden deaths as a result of, for example, road traffic accidents or heart attacks. In these circumstances, professionals are faced with different challenges when working with the children. Breaking the news to the children is explored, as is the process for saying goodbye. There is also a discussion about the period following the death; this relates especially to when circumstances dictate that a post-mortem is required and there is an extended period between the death and the funeral. The chapter concludes with a section focusing on the availability of support for professionals. Acknowledgement is given to the emotionally complex role professionals have when working with children who are experiencing the death of a parent, and the strain that this can place on them professionally and personally. Time is spent reflecting on how stress can manifest itself in an individual, along with some suggestions for stress management.

It seems appropriate that one of the final destinations in the book is the support and welfare of the practitioner. After all, their role is vital in facilitating and developing conversations with children about parental terminal illness and death. Being confident and competent in communicating with this population of children is really important, but so too is taking care of oneself. Fellow travellers not only need to know the terrain well – they also need to be emotionally agile to traverse the alien landscape if they are going to be effective in their roles.

Chapter 2

The Importance of Communication

Communication is fundamental to all work with service users, whether this is in the briefest of interactions or a complex assessment. Without communication very little can be achieved: the worker is ineffective and the service user left feeling let down by the system. Within all professions the quality of communication exchanges will have a significant bearing on how the relationship between service user and worker develops and how the work proceeds. Furthermore, communication between colleagues and other professionals is also vital in the development of effective practice. This was highlighted in Lord Laming's (2003) report following the death of Victoria Climbié where the focus of major recommendations concerned communication within and between agencies. The importance of good communication skills when working with children cannot be over-emphasised and, when this work relates to parental terminal illness, the quality of the interactions is especially important.

Talking to children about parental terminal illness can be unmistakably difficult emotionally. It is the type of conversation that we hope never to have in either our personal or professional lives and yet statistically such conversations need to be held regularly. It is estimated that 50 children per day will experience the death of a parent (Stokes 2004) and, while this figure includes sudden and traumatic death, it remains probable that a significant percentage of these children will be experiencing death from terminal illness. Research consistently shows how imperative it is for children to be prepared and informed about what is happening within their family, in order to ensure that the frightening alien landscape of parental terminal illness and death is navigated as smoothly and easily as possible (Christ 2000a; Christ and Christ 2006; Fearnley 2010; Rauch *et al.* 2002).

When working with children whose parents are terminally ill, there are often limited opportunities to develop the work and to undertake ongoing sessions. Chowns highlights this when she writes 'pre-bereavement work has to contend with one major and unique issue – uncertainty' (2005, p.125). She is referring here to the difficulties in knowing whether the ill parents are going to respond to treatment or whether they will die, and when this will happen. These are factors that create circumstances where there is sometimes only one opportunity to meet and talk with the children; however, ideally with time, planning and consideration, a number of sessions can be arranged. Furthermore, other constraints sometimes mean that opportunities to work with children are lost. All members of the multi-disciplinary team need to take responsibility in recognising and acknowledging when there are children in the family, and in working towards supporting those children. Early assessment of the patient, whereby family members are identified, is the first step to ensuring that there is sufficient time available to work with the children. Research has shown that typically there remains an unspoken assumption that the patient's needs are paramount, at the expense of other family members' needs (Dunning 2006). While it is difficult to argue that the patient's needs are not paramount, a wider perspective should be adopted where the children are recognised as being in need of help and support during this difficult period. Whether the opportunities for spending time communicating with the children are limited to one-off sessions, or more comprehensive sessions can be facilitated, being aware of and having an understanding of different forms of communication is a positive starting point when working with these children.

Within this chapter different types of communication will be discussed. These include spoken communication, listening, non-verbal communication and communication through the written word. The value of these different forms will be explored in the context of practice. I will then briefly describe children's development in relation to their growing understanding of dying and death. This will be followed by a discussion about the different sources from which children garner their knowledge, and the role professionals have in this. Finally, the rhetorical question, 'What do you communicate when you do not communicate?' will be posed and the problems of not communicating with children discussed.

The forms of communication typically employed

The term 'communication' is very broad and often used as a catch-all for any interactions encountered by two or more people. It 'involves a process in which a message is transmitted from a communicator to a receiver' (Reith and Payne 2009, p.43). Two fundamental forms of communication are speech and listening, although frequently the latter is given scant attention or acknowledgement. However, if how we communicate is explored in more detail, it becomes apparent that speech and listening are both very wide-ranging categories and there are many elements to both of them. There is a range of ways in which communication occurs, and, in this ever-rapidly changing world where communication highways are developing at a great pace, different opportunities are coming to the fore. Today communication across the globe can occur at the push of a button; information can be exchanged instantly and to a worldwide audience. However, in this world of multi-media communication, the 'grass-roots' work of professionals communicating face to face with service users remains as necessary and important as it always has been.

Spoken communication

The most common form of communication is spoken communication. Very few interactions take place without some language being spoken. But how the words are spoken, what words are uttered and the tone of voice all play a significant role in how the interactions develop, as do the accompanying body language and facial expressions. Furthermore, professionals always need to be conscious of the language they are adopting. Is it age appropriate, is jargon being used that may confuse children, is English the children's first language, do the children have developmental delay that affects their communication or how they cognitively process information?

Communicating through age-appropriate language is the basis of good professional practice and should be the bedrock of all interactions with children. This is never truer than when talking to them about parental terminal illness. Adopting the correct level and employing language that is suitable to the age and development of a child helps in creating an atmosphere where the communication exchanges can be most effective. It is important to recognise and acknowledge that when engaging in difficult conversations children's ability to process the content of the discussions may be altered or impaired. Furthermore, the content is of paramount importance to the children concerned and likely to be a constant companion in their lives. Engaging with a worker who understands this and who can enter discussions that are meaningful and easily understandable will help them in the process of attempting to make sense of a situation that may seem incomprehensible.

Finding the right words to use is often difficult when anticipating conversations with these children and it can be tempting to slip into the safe professional world of jargon. In this protected world, workers can display an air of confidence and authority that masks their true feelings of uncertainty and hesitance. However, this practice only serves to increase the children's anxiety and leads to further misunderstandings and confusion. The use, or misuse, of jargon is discussed in more detail in Chapter 3 when some of the typical barriers to communicating are explored.

The tone of voice used can convey a very clear message to the people being spoken to and can affect how they receive the information being given. Children are particularly receptive to tone of voice and may filter out what is actually being said in favour of 'hearing' the tone. Children, especially younger ones, often associate different tones with warnings, advisory statements and being told off. Some of the first encounters babies and toddlers have with language include 'Don't touch', 'Don't go near there', 'No', and more often than not these statements are said in a tone of voice that has some urgency and harshness for effect. It is therefore probable to assume that when children are being given information, as they decode what is being said, the tone of voice will be influential in their thinking and thus their assimilation of the information. Children who are living with the knowledge that their parent is dying are likely to be hypersensitive to any opportunities they encounter where information is being shared about the illness or issues that are affecting their lives. As a consequence, they are likely to interpret the tone of voice as being symbolic of the information being shared.

Chunking the information

As with all professional communication, pacing the exchange between the individuals concerned is also imperative for effective communication to take place. The term 'pacing' refers to giving the information and communicating at a suitable and appropriate pace for the service user. It may mean giving chunks of information in small bursts and also repeating the content of the exchange over a period. Providing small chunks helps recipients to absorb what is being said and enables them to begin making sense of the information. Thinking about communication in terms of a process and not a one-off event is helpful (Christ 2000a).

Conversations with patients and their carers are ideally paced over a period of time to allow them to absorb the information that is being given. This practice enables them to assimilate what they are being told, process the information and ask questions. The same approach should be taken with children. They too need to be told things more than once and possibly in different ways to allow them to begin to understand and work through what is being said and the information that is being given.

Sometimes it is unavoidable that the worker only gets one opportunity to meet with and talk to the children. This is often the situation in emergency and trauma-related cases, but sadly it is also all too often the case within palliative care settings. The focus of care is on the patient and the psychosocial and emotional needs of the children are not prioritised or in some cases even considered important or necessary. It is in these situations, when it is apparent that the parent is going to die imminently, that a worker may be called upon to 'talk' to the children about what is happening. In these situations, it is very difficult to build up any relationship with the children, and how the conversation is approached is different from the preferred style where time, albeit limited, is available.

When talking with children about their parent's illness and death, the ideal situation is one where the worker is able to spend time getting to know them and to develop a trusting relationship. The children need to know that the worker is someone they can confide in and who will respond to their questions, fears, hopes and thoughts without judgement and with honesty. Pacing the discussions means that the children are not taking in too much information at once; instead they are being given small chunks of information that they can assimilate and process before receiving more. Taking in, understanding and beginning to accept such difficult conversations takes time and the children will need to revisit what has been said over and over. It is also important here that the information given can be built on and solidified to maximise understanding. Being able to revisit the communication exchange over time, and as the illness develops and the parent's health deteriorates, helps children to cement their understanding of what is happening and through this begin to make meaning from the situation.

Pacing the conversations

In line with all good professional practice, it is important that the conversations are structured so that the children have some control in determining the pace of the discussions. Being given the opportunity to change the topic of conversation, slow down the exchange or 'fast forward' to another part of the discussion allows them to manage more effectively a situation where they have very little control. For children living with a parent who is dying, it often feels as though their worlds are going to implode imminently and that they have absolutely no control over what is unfolding in their lives. Therefore, having opportunities to explore their feelings at their own pace, and being able to make decisions about how the conversations progress, is important for them.

How information is given – some practicalities

How information is given to children and the process of engaging with them are hugely significant in enabling them to begin to make some sense of what is happening and to start the process of meaning making.

Vignette

Sally, a cheery six-year-old, has recently become quieter and her behaviour has altered. Sally's mother has terminal cancer and is now receiving palliative care; she has been told by her oncologist that she has probably got less than a month to live. Following the initial diagnosis, the family decided not to tell Sally about her mother's illness. However, because of the imminent death they feel that she should be told. They ask the Macmillan nurse for help and she agrees to meet with Sally after school. The nurse has little time at the visit because of the pressure of work and the need to get to another appointment. She meets with Sally and introduces her to a book written especially for children about dying and death. The nurse reads the book to Sally and leaves a copy for the family. After reading the book together, the nurse tells Sally that, like the little girl in the book, her mummy is very poorly and, even though the nurses and doctors have tried to make her better, they think that she might not get better and will die.

Exercise

How might Sally be left feeling? What could the nurse have done differently in such a small amount of time?

Observations of the vignette

It is likely that Sally will be left feeling very confused, alone and afraid after this encounter. She has been thrown into a situation with someone she does not know, given emotionally saturated information and then left to process what she has been told. She has no support available from her family and therefore no one with whom to discuss what she has just learnt. The passing on of information has been done quickly in one huge chunk with no consideration of Sally's needs. The lack of pacing means that she is unable to assimilate the information or begin to process what she has heard. The content of the story book has not been explained to her and she has not been given the opportunity to discuss what she has been told or to ask questions.

Finding the right time to talk

Related to the pacing of the communication exchanges is the topic of timing. One participant in my research (Fearnley 2010) candidly observed that there will never be a 'right time' to talk to children about their parent's death along with all the associated factors that are highly likely to affect their lives. As adults we tend instinctively to protect children from anything that is likely to upset, disturb or hurt them, and as a result it is easy to put off those conversations that we would rather not have. There is always likely to be a little voice at the back of our minds telling us that we cannot say anything now because they are about to go to school or they have just come home from school or it is homework time or it is the weekend or it is Monday morning. The excuses are endless but to put off telling children has the potential to be severely damaging to them.

The communication environment

Being in a 'safe' environment is very important. Children need to feel that they can express their feelings safely and away from other observers. Whether the work is undertaken in the family's home or at another location is dependent on a number of factors. The family may have a strong preference about where any work takes place; some may request that it is undertaken in the home while others may feel it is more appropriate to be in a 'neutral' environment. If it is within a hospital or hospice, care and consideration needs to be given to whereabouts it is undertaken. The ward or by the parent's bedside may not be an appropriate location. Such situations rarely offer any privacy (for the children, their parents and other patients) and the setting could be seen as being very clinical and a false environment for the children. Ideally there should be a room available where the worker and children can meet without being disturbed and where the children will feel safe.

Sessions with children should not be restricted to being held within buildings. A walk in the local park or even an outing to the shops can provide a rich environment where opportunities to talk and explore the situation can be available. The distractions of window shopping or playing on the swings can be the perfect place for children to relax and be themselves for a brief period. This is an important consideration when thinking about the children's needs. Living constantly with the uncertainty and all the changes that parental terminal illness brings means that being able to escape, albeit for a short period, gives the children the opportunity to revert back briefly to their familiar lives before illness entered the family. It is important therefore that we respect this need and acknowledge that we will not necessarily complete all the work that we had planned! Being away from the situation can also mean that the children relax and are able to explore their feelings. It is noteworthy, too, that in these less formal settings the children may not appear to be processing what is being said, but they are likely to be assimilating more than we recognise.

Sometimes opportune moments arrive that had neither been planned for nor anticipated. Car journeys are a prime example where children, as the passengers, often instigate conversations. But equally this time travelling often presents the worker with a valuable opportunity to have a meaningful discussion with children. I have had numerous such discussions when transporting children (and adults) and have come to the conclusion that within the confines of a car, where, as the driver you are concentrating on driving, the children feel safe to talk. In such situations it is difficult to have eye contact with each other and it is therefore potentially less threatening.

There will be situations and occasions where children initiate the conversation and the worker then needs to be prepared to respond appropriately. As with all work with children, it is important to recognise that their agendas for talking may not be congruent with the worker's. Initiating discussions about painful and very personal issues will not always occur at prescribed times. Children, and their emotions, are not automated devices that function at the push of a button. It is also true that children may take every available opportunity to avoid any conversations. Some children will choose not to talk about what is happening. This can be seen by adults as their denying what is happening, but often it is a coping strategy that is vital and again gives them some control over the situation. This will be explored in detail in Chapter 4.

Different mediums for communicating

The telephone can, occasionally, be a useful medium for communication. Older children particularly may use the opportunity to talk about their situation using the telephone. Sometimes it may be that they have thought about something that is important and they need to explore, or they may feel that asking questions in the presence of family members is not appropriate. Therefore, being able to telephone a worker is a valuable opportunity: it offers some distance between the two parties and gives the children a modicum of control over the situation. They can terminate the conversation at any given point and can direct where it leads. Additionally the telephone provides a very effective barrier: the person on the other end of the line cannot see facial expressions or body language and, therefore, some degree of privacy can be maintained. However, a word of caution needs to be offered. While telephone conversations are helpful when a relationship between the children and the worker has been established, the telephone should never be used to replace face-to-face discussions when the initial discussions about the illness and prognosis are being shared. While this may seem to be a safe option for workers and offer them a protective barrier between themselves and the children, it would be totally inappropriate, unprofessional and poor practice to discuss such difficult information via the telephone.

Mind your language – euphemisms

Language, and how it is used, is incredibly powerful. The language adopted when communicating with children about their parent's illness strongly influences how they begin to make sense of what is happening, or conversely how they make mis-meaning from the situation. Using age-appropriate language and being careful not to slip into professional jargon are two important elements that need to be considered when communicating with children, but equally important is the avoidance of euphemistic language. Euphemisms are defined as 'an inoffensive word or phrase substituted for one considered offensive or hurtful' (Collins 1995). Words associated with dying, death and bereavement are often substituted and whether this is to 'protect' the conveyer or the recipient is open to question. What is very clear, however, is that adopting such language has the real potential to severely affect children's understanding of the situation.

There is an abundance of euphemisms that are regularly used, for example:

- 'She has got the big C.'
- 'gone to sleep'
- 'gone to another room'
- 'returned to the pavilion'
- 'We have lost grandpa.'

Exercise

Think about other euphemisms that you have used in your professional and personal life. Is this usage a conscious decision or is it part of your culture?

It is often thought that by replacing the words 'dying' and 'dead' for the 'safer' euphemisms, the enormity of the meaning of the words is being cushioned. It was once explained to me that euphemisms 'soften' the harshness of the situation. Adults may find comfort in being protected from the reality of what is happening, but when children are confronted with such language it generally only causes confusion and severe misunderstandings that inhibit their ability to make sense of what is unfolding.

Vignette

During a visit to see her mother, Sally hears that another patient on the ward 'has gone to sleep' and witnesses hushed conversations and much distress. Sally is aware that the patient is no longer on the ward and that something has happened to her. Over the following few nights, Sally's sleep pattern becomes disturbed: she refuses to sleep in her own bed, insisting that she sleeps in her father's bedroom. During the night she wakes her father on a number of occasions requesting a drink and help to go to the lavatory. This is a significant change in Sally's behaviour and is out of character. In addition, when Sally visited her mother and her mother was sleeping, Sally twice deliberately woke her mother 'because I've got something important to tell you'. Sally's father became increasingly annoyed by her behaviour and it was only during a casual conversation with the ward sister that the problem was discussed. Through this discussion it emerged that Sally had heard about the patient 'going to sleep'. The ward sister made the connection between this information and the changes in Sally's behaviour. The euphemism had become entrenched in her literal mind and had spread fear and anxiety.

Observations of the vignette

The dramatic changes to Sally's behaviour exemplify how the choice of language needs to be carefully thought through, and highlight the consequences of inappropriate language. If children are told or overhear that, for example, someone has 'gone to sleep', this is likely to create anxiety and raise questions such as 'If they have gone to sleep, why can't I go and wake them up?' or 'If I go to bed tonight and fall asleep, will the same thing happen to me?' This then raises anxieties about sleep and can be related, by the children, not only to their own sleep patterns but also to those of their family and friends. If a child is living with the knowledge that their parent is seriously ill and then makes the connection about 'going to sleep', a natural reaction is for them to try everything possible to prevent the parent from resting, just as Sally did with her mother.

Exercise

Look at the following euphemisms and commonly used phrases; think about how they could be interpreted by children and the possible consequences of their mis-meanings:

- 'God has taken him to be an angel because he was so good.'
- 'He has passed away.'
- 'Daddy went on a long journey and he won't be coming back.'
- 'She went into hospital and died.'

Dunning (2006) provides some wonderful examples of how children have misinterpreted what they have been told or heard, and the consequences of such mistakes. These include the five-year-old who refused to eat his normal breakfast food. This was because he heard on the television about a 'serial killer'. When I have used Dunning's examples during training sessions, they have always been greeted with humour and an 'Ah bless' response. But while they may have brought some laughter and light relief to what are serious sessions, they too highlight the importance of the language used and also the necessity of checking out children's understanding.

The professionals working with children and their families need to be mindful of the effect language can have on children's understanding. They need to be aware of their own language and reflect good practice in the words that they use, but also to be mindful of the language of colleagues and, if necessary, challenge their discourse. When working alongside families, professionals need to listen to the language adopted by them. If the communication culture within the family is such that euphemisms are part of the discourse, it may be advisable to explore, very gently, with the parents the possible negative outcomes of such usage and to think together of alternative language.

Listening

There is often a discrepancy between listening to children and actually hearing what they are saying. As professionals we all purport to listen to our service users but do we always hear what they say?

Vignette

Following the initial session with the Macmillan nurse, Sally is frequently seen on the ward by the staff. The Macmillan nurse briefly discussed Sally at the multi-disciplinary team meeting and now all the team are aware that she is visiting her mother regularly. During one visit Sally is busy colouring in her book when the social worker passes by the bed. The social worker comments on her colouring and Sally responds, 'Yes I am a good girl now.' As Sally makes this comment, she selects the black felt-tip pen and scribbles furiously over the drawing.

Observations of the vignette

Listening to Sally, the social worker hears her claim that she is 'a good girl now' and takes comfort that the session with the Macmillan nurse has been helpful. However, did the social worker actually hear Sally? Was her comment a glib answer to the comments about her colouring or was she conveying far more than was interpreted? What was Sally's tone of voice and was her behaviour – for example, with the black crayon – congruent with what she was saying?

Being attuned to children's conversations is a skill that takes time to develop. However, it is an important skill to nurture because actually hearing what children are saying is different from listening to them. Lefevre (2010) reminds her readers about the importance of really listening to children. She is relating this specifically to social work practice but her assertions are transferrable to all professionals working with children. Writing about child protection work, Lefevre states that 'children are often too powerless, traumatised, confused or frightened to speak directly about such matters: they may also lack the conceptual understanding or vocabulary to do so' (2010, p.36). This is equally valid for children experiencing the death of a parent. Living with parental terminal illness can traumatise children. It is certainly a confusing and frightening period in their lives and, without appropriate and consistent communication, they are likely to lack the conceptual understanding to begin to make sense of what is happening. Lefevre states that children expect that the professionals working with them '*should* be able to listen' (2010, p.36, emphasis added). Offering a tokenistic 'ear' will give children a very strong message that they are peripheral in what is happening and that their needs are not as important as the adults around them.

Actually attending to the words, and trying to decode them, allows us then to explore in more detail the lexical meaning. Children are gifted in knowing and being able to say what they want the adults around them to hear. However, they will also say what they think the adults want to hear.

There are many reasons why professionals do not always listen attentively to conversations with service users. The demands of work are often such that too many competing pressures are placed on them and their capacity to attend to the present is lost under the weight of focusing on heavy caseloads. Not having time to actually listen can compromise effectiveness and have a severe impact on the work being undertaken. However, being afraid to 'hear' the conversations is a more problematic reason for not listening to service users and this can have serious consequences. Barriers to communicating with children will be considered in detail in the next chapter.

Non-verbal communication

The focus so far has been on verbal communication; however, the importance of non-verbal communication, both the worker's and the children's, must not be overlooked. Body language encompasses many nuances, all of which have the potential to send powerful messages. I recall, with shame, many years ago as a young nursery nurse, being quite rightly reprimanded for the body language I had employed when, in the middle of the children's lunches, a father brought his child into the room for the afternoon session. The child was struggling to settle into his new routine of nursery life and I was aware that integrating him into the session was going to be time consuming when we also had to attend to the other children's meals. My verbal language was welcoming; however, my body language was apparently anything but and gave a strong message to the father who expressed his concerns to my manager. An avoidable and unnecessary lesson was learned that day but one that has stayed with me throughout my career. The adage 'actions speak louder than words' could be equally translated into 'non-verbal communication speaks louder than words'!

It is especially important when trying to communicate difficult or painful information that our non-verbal communication is carefully monitored. Our own anxieties and feelings of discomfort may seep out through non-verbal communication and children will intuitively respond to these messages.

Non-verbal communication includes a plethora of facial expressions that can transmit very clear messages to children. A smile can convey warmth and empathy and be a signal for friendly encounters but in slightly different circumstances it can also be viewed as a symbol of irony and insincerity, especially when accompanied with a small shrug of the shoulders. Laughing with service users transmits the message of brief shared humour, but it can also be translated as a sarcastic response to their comments or even a clear dismissal of their opinions and views.

To have eye contact or not

The use of eye contact can be difficult to manage. While, in British culture, eye contact is seen as a sign of being trustworthy, sometimes there is a balance to be achieved, especially when working with children. For some children, sitting face to face and having to make eye contact is disconcerting and creates feelings of unease. This relates back to the earlier discussions about the positive distractions that travelling in a car can present. Here there are few expectations to engage in face-to-face discussions where giving eye contact would be the norm. Therefore, children are indirectly given permission not to follow cultural norms and expectations. Professionals need to recognise this and acknowledge that the children's behaviour is not disrespectful but rather an adaptive coping strategy that offers them some control and comfort in a difficult situation.

Are you sitting comfortably?

How professionals sit and their body posture when working with children can transmit to them very powerful subconscious messages. Electing to sit in a chair, or remaining standing, while the children are sitting on the floor sends a strong message about power and control.

However, if workers ask the children where they would like them to sit, this ensures that they are being given choice and some control in the situation. If, because of mobility difficulties, sitting on the floor would be problematic, it is prudent for workers to mention this to the children and to explain succinctly why they are not sitting alongside them. Giving children choice about where they would like the workers to sit or stand during the session is also a way of demonstrating respect and is always good practice. When workers opt to sit behind their desk, this not only creates a physical barrier but an emotional and psychological one too.

What is your body language saying?

The worker's body language during sessions with children also sends strong messages to them. When discussing parental illness and death, if workers are not comfortable and confident, their own feelings of discomfort are likely to surface. Feeling unsure of what to say and being worried that the discussions will make the situation 'worse' are factors that can contribute to these feelings of unease. However, to be effective in the work and to offer the best possible support to children, being comfortable with death and not being 'death denying' are hugely important elements. The slightest feelings of anxiety or unease are likely to be transmitted through body language. Twitching and fiddling with jewellery or the note pad, which is so often the worker's comfort blanket, are signs of being uncomfortable and unhappy with the situation. These behaviours could be sending two interrelated messages to the children. The first is that the worker is not really interested in them or what is being discussed, but the second and probably more insidious message is that the situation really is awful and the worker is trying to protect them from the reality of what is happening. Of course the situation is awful; it is likely to be the most difficult situation the children have ever been required to cope with, but with the correct support they do generally have the resilience to deal with what is happening.

Professionals need to be cognisant not only of their body language and the messages they are transmitting, but also of the children's. Is their non-verbal communication and body language congruent with their spoken language? They may be stating that they are 'okay' and yet their posture and non-verbal behaviour tell another story. Sally's behaviour with the crayons told a different story from the one she was telling the social worker.

Written communication

The final forms of communication to be discussed are those that are written. Written communication, in whatever form, can provide a lasting testament to what is being said. Therefore, careful consideration needs to be given to the content of the communication – after all, what is written can remain with the recipient for a lifetime.

Letter writing

Writing a brief letter or card to children following an emotionally saturated session provides a form of continuation and shows a respect for them and the work undertaken. The note only needs to be brief, containing possibly a short summary of the session along with observations of what happened. (For a helpful introduction to writing therapeutic letters, see Freeman, Epston and Lobovits 1997). The note should be written in age-appropriate language and be 'child friendly'. Before sending any mail, it is good practice to ask the children whether they would be happy to receive post. The family circumstances may be such that for them to receive mail may cause conflict or jeopardise the nature of the work. It is also important to think about their literacy levels. Receiving a letter when they are not confident readers or have limited literacy would be likely to be unhelpful.

The use of email

Corresponding via the Internet is also now an option. Emails are an instant form of communication (Baym 2010) and an ongoing dialogue can be developed. If this is a form of preferred communication, it is advisable to explain to the children that any responses made to their emails are likely to be determined by a worker's time constraints and pressures at work. If children finally find the courage to email a sensitive question about their current situation or make an observation about their lives, it can be very disheartening to keep checking the inbox and finding no reply. It is also vitally important that, if promises are made to correspond, whether by letter or email, these promises are kept. In the turbulent world of parental terminal illness, where all routines and patterns of life are fractured, broken promises from professionals only add to the feelings of insecurity and being alone.

Text messaging

Keeping in contact between sessions with text messages can again be a positive way of maintaining an ongoing relationship with the children. However, it is again important that this form of communication is acceptable to them. When discussing it with them, it should be highlighted that the text message may be received when they are at school or out with friends. Some children prefer not to impart the information about their parent's illness to friends and peers, and consequently receiving a text could compromise their ability to maintain their preferred identity with peers. Again it is important to think about the content of these text messages. They should remain neutral salutations and not become substitutes for conventional support or therapeutic sessions.

When communicating with children, in whatever form, their cognitive and emotional development needs to be considered. Children's concepts of dying and death take time to develop and are significant factors when workers are thinking about how most effectively to communicate with them. The following section provides a brief overview of children's development in relation to their understanding of dying and death.

Children's development

How children begin to attempt to make some meaning from the situation they are thrown into is dependent on a number of factors. The extent of communication and information sharing and the level of honesty about the situation that their parents provide are of paramount importance in helping children, of whatever age, to start to navigate the alien landscape of parental terminal illness. Professionals play a vital role in helping to facilitate these conversations and also in developing their own conversations with children. However, the children's age and development are significant factors in determining how they cognitively process the information and how the communication exchanges take place. For example, how a three-year-old conceptualises and processes what is happening, and from this how they begin to make some meaning from the situation, will be very different from how a 15-year-old does this.

Three- to five-year-olds

Young preschool-aged children begin to understand that something within their family is wrong but are not yet able to comprehend the permanence of death (Christ and Christ 2006). Moreover, children of this age tend to adopt magical thinking, whereby they wrongly attribute their thoughts or actions as being causal in the development of the illness. Adults listening to children therefore need to be 'tuned in' to their thought processes so that they can understand more clearly what they are saying and what they actually mean. Their limited vocabulary and developing cognitive processes mean that they often struggle to express their feelings verbally. This age group of children will therefore use other outlets to express their feelings and emotions, including play, drawings and behaviour. It is therefore important to recognise, when working with this age group, that it would be insufficient just to talk about what is happening. The children would benefit from opportunities to explore their feelings expressively through play or artwork. Moreover, giving this age group of children chunks of information, in very simple language, is crucial.

Six- to eight-year-olds

Children in the six- to eight-year-old group are still likely to demonstrate illogical and magical thinking when attempting to make some sense of what is happening. However, unlike the younger age group, their development is such that they are able to begin to anticipate the death as the illness progresses. Three types of information are therefore helpful when communicating with this age group:

- simple, concrete information about the disease, including its name, how it progresses, the symptoms, treatments and causes

- simple explanations about the patient's behaviour and their appearance in relation to the symptoms and treatment of the disease

- being informed when death is imminent.

(Christ and Christ 2006, p.203)

When this information is being shared, it is important that the children's understanding is constantly being monitored. Have they interpreted correctly what they have been told? Checking out and asking them to describe their interpretation of what has been said is helpful here.

Nine- to eleven-year-olds

Between the ages of nine and eleven, children are developmentally at a stage where they are beginning to be able to use logical thinking and understand cause and effect. Because of this, it is helpful to provide them with detailed information about the illness and treatment, thus enabling them to begin to understand what is happening and have some sense of control. The value of continually providing small chunks of information is again helpful and assists them in beginning to make some meaning of what is happening. As with the younger age groups, the use of art, craft and play is helpful when working with these children.

Twelve- to fourteen-year-olds

Within this period children begin to understand the full implications of the seriousness of the crisis within their family but they still have difficulty managing their emotions about the loss. For children of this age, there is a dichotomy between the need to withdraw emotionally from their family and the need to respond to the crisis within it. Erikson (1963) describes the adolescent period as being a time of identity crisis where young people need to find a definition of who they are while at the same time dealing with the upheaval and confusion that is often associated with this period. If young people also need to manage the upheaval of living with a parent who is dying, they are forced into coping with additional stressors that can severely compromise their definition of self. Barnes *et al.* (1998) argue that these issues are compounded for children who have a learning disability. They assert that during this developmental period the task of moving towards individualisation is more complex for children who have a disability because of their heightened dependence, for all aspects of their care, on their primary carers.

Children in Christ's (2000a) research stated that they had been adequately informed about what was happening and, moreover, that they understood what was occurring. However, they tended to indicate that they did not necessarily want information about what was happening. Interestingly though, in an earlier study of mothers with breast cancer, the same age group of children indicated that they wanted more specific illness-related information than they were receiving (Lewis 1990). This discrepancy illustrates the need to be cognisant of the needs of individual children and the importance of not stereotyping them together as one homogeneous group.

Fifteen and older

Older children show a more adult-like maturity to their thinking and understanding of illness and consequently tend to enjoy more open conversations about what is happening. However, they are also likely to be struggling with philosophical questions about their identity; therefore, the crisis of parental terminal illness has the potential to destabilise what is already a turbulent period in their lives. Their more mature status can be misread by adults and, as a consequence, they can be provided with too much information at once or not offered any information because of the erroneous belief that they know what is happening and are fully aware of everything.

This brief resume of children's development and their understanding of dying and death should not be generalised. It is important to remember that each child is an individual and that different factors will contribute to each one's level of understanding. Children with a learning disability that affects their cognitive development, or who have communication difficulties, are likely to experience additional problems in their attempts to make meaning of what is happening. Likewise, children whose first language is not English will require additional support, and cultural aspects will also need to be considered. Entering the alien landscape of parental terminal illness is such that all children, of whatever age, may display some regression in their development. However, if this is handled sensitively and they are given appropriate support, it will only be a temporary regression.

The extent of children's knowledge about a situation

There is the old saying that 'a little knowledge is a dangerous thing' and this is very true when considering children, parental terminal illness, and communication and information sharing. Incomplete knowledge or information that is 'economical with the truth' can lead to misinterpretations and misunderstandings that are particularly unhelpful when children are trying to make some meaning of a seemingly meaningless situation.

Where children get their knowledge from

Being given accurate information is crucial to children to help them navigate the alien landscape of parental terminal illness, but where do they get this information from? Parents are ideally the primary providers of information and should be seen as the constant variables in the exchanges. Parents are generally best placed to talk with their children: they know their children and have a developed communication system in place. The parents, or close family members, are the people who have most contact with their children even if, as so often is the case, family life is taken up with treatment regimes, medical appointments or hospital visits. The well parent is still likely to have more contact with the children than any professional. However, frequently the magnitude of the family crisis gets in the way of these conversations taking place and, as we shall see in Chapter 3, barriers are often prevalent.

The professional's role

Professionals working with a family have a significant role to play in supporting the parents to have conversations with their children. They can often introduce an objective perspective and, through this, facilitate discussions initiated by the parents. The professionals' knowledge, gained from both research and practice, can offer a different dimension that helps the parents to think about the value of talking to the children about what is happening. Additionally, the professionals have an important role in communicating directly with the children. Being able to talk to someone who is not intimately involved with the situation may allow the children to explore their feelings and thoughts from a different perspective and within the context of a safe environment. Children will frequently avoid talking to their parents about the situation for fear of upsetting them. They often feel that their parents have enough to cope with without having to be burdened by their worries. Therefore, the professionals become that 'safe pair of ears' and are likely to be perceived as safe confidants with whom the children can share their fears, anxieties and hopes. Moreover, professionals can provide a different, objective perspective. They can offer a more detached overview and act as neutral people for the children who often see them as the ones with all the knowledge and experience to help them make some meaning of the situation.

Media and telecommunications

Recent technological advancements enable children to access information from sources that a few years ago were unheard of. The

Internet can be a valuable resource and provide much information about an illness, its trajectory, treatment and outcomes. However, the information will be general and not specific to individual circumstances; it may therefore provide an alternative, inaccurate story that can lead to false hope and once again misinformation. Alternatively, accessing such information could create considerable fear in children and again cause them to misunderstand what is happening within their family and to their parent. Furthermore, accessing the Internet can be a private activity and thus a responsible 'knowing' adult may not be policing the information the children are accessing or filtering out inappropriate or unhelpful material. Resources such as the Internet can have a part to play in informing children, but they should only be used to supplement the more direct face-to-face information exchanges that are so important and necessary.

An alternative way to gain insights into issues of dying and death is through the media and popular television programmes. However, the portrayal of such important themes is generally focused towards sensationalising the event for maximum effect (Cox, Garrett and Graham 2004–2005). Therefore, if a child's information has mainly come from such external sources, their knowledge of dying and death, and their only available discourses, are likely to be inaccurate, sensationalised and probably horrific. Professionals need to be aware, when working with children, that they may have developed cognitions about their current situation from sources that might not be accurate and might have been grossly generalised. This erroneous information is then likely to influence their thinking and affect the meaning-making process. Therefore, having an understanding about what children already know and how they have interpreted information is important when planning work with them. It may be necessary to spend time undoing the knowledge that has been gained so that a more accurate account can be developed.

Books – the font of all information?

Books about death are now becoming more widely available for children. Some of these are factual books while others are from within the fiction genre. Before directing children to these books, the worker should always read them first to check for content and accuracy. Many of the books aimed at younger readers use the death of a pet or an inanimate character as the principal story line. Although these books offer an introduction about dying and death, they also have the potential to misrepresent issues of parental death and the realities that children typically experience. Often the story is about the death of a pet; the child character mourns the death but then buys a replacement. Christ (2000b) points out that young children (three- to five-year-olds), shortly after the death of a parent, will ask the surviving parent to find a replacement. If their cognitions are reinforced with story books where replacements are easily accessible, their meaning-making process is likely to be poorly informed and this will lead to additional, unnecessary upset.

'Stolen conversations'

When thinking about practice and communicating with children, it is advisable never to underestimate how much information the children are likely to glean from listening to 'stolen conversations'. These could be from overheard conversations at home, hushed and quickly snatched telephone conversations between concerned adults, or playground discussions. Although children often try to avoid imparting information about their parent's illness to friends, it is frequently the situation that friends know more about what is happening than they do. Friends' parents may have shared in 'school gate' discussions about the ill parent and then repeated these conversations at home.

When children glean information about their parent's illness from indirect sources, it is often inaccurate and patchy. Moreover, when they learn about their parent's illness from sources other than their parents, there are a number of implications that need to be recognised. The children are likely to feel betrayed that the trust they had in their parents has been compromised and that they have not been party to a significant family secret. Furthermore, these stolen conversations can lead to children drawing their own conclusions about what is happening. Putting two and two together and making six is not unusual when only limited and inaccurate information is available. Moreover, because magical thinking is a feature, particularly in early childhood, incomplete information may lead to more erroneous ideas being constructed. Therefore, it may be valuable to gently offer these examples to parents who are reluctant to engage in conversations with their children. It will highlight to them the importance of giving accurate 'first-hand' as opposed to potentially inaccurate 'second-hand' information.

Finding out what children know, or think they know

It is important, when preparing to work with children, that as much information is obtained about what they already know. A starting point when undertaking the work is to ask, 'Tell me what you think is happening in your family at the moment.' This opens up the communication exchange and allows the worker to make an assessment of the level and detail of the knowledge and understanding that the children have about the illness and prognosis.

Styles of working and especially communication styles will affect how the relationship between worker and child develops. Children, who have been on the periphery of their parent's illness and have observed all the interactions with the different professionals involved, may equate professionals' involvement with them as being closely connected to their parent's medical care. If this is the situation, they may find it difficult to begin engaging with them. To them professionals are those people who cause their mummy or daddy to have pain, when they give them injections or when they see them in the hospital or hospice. If their role is such that they nurse or care for the patient along with working with the children, it is important that these roles are differentiated. This then allows the children to understand that the time spent with a professional is for them – it is their 'protected' time, not a supplement to their parent's care.

Practice point

Throughout the process of communicating with children, an important element to remember is that how and what is communicated with them has the potential to have a lasting effect on how they cope with and manage the situation both before their parent dies and into the bereavement period.

What do you communicate when you do not communicate?

Communication, in whatever form, has the power to give very strong messages. How a message is interpreted is open to a number of translations. The context of the situation, past experiences, and personal cultures and beliefs will contribute to decoding the information and drawing conclusions about what is being said. But what do we communicate when we do not communicate? The old adage 'no news is good news' is true in many situations but could also mean that something important is being hidden.

The lives of children living with a parent who is dying are thrown into chaos and confusion. All the predictable, known routines in life are turned upside down with the arrival of a diagnosis of a terminal illness. Weber, Rowling and Scanlon suggest that 'human beings are more than processors of information and experience; they are also constructors of meaning' (2007, p.947). Therefore, if children are not included in conversations about what is happening, very strong messages about what is occurring are being transmitted. When we do not communicate, we invariably communicate strong messages that, as we have already seen, can cause children to place their own meaning on what is happening. However, more often than not, these meanings and interpretations are inaccurate because of the lack of available correct information. Furthermore, in order to have some control over the situation, the children need to understand what is happening and why (Weber *et al.* 2007).

By not communicating with children, whether this is from a genuine belief that too much information may harm their well-being or because of their own fears and lack of skills, professionals are sending a very clear message that something is not right. Along with forming their own interpretations, children also begin to question their identity and positioning in the family. Their exclusion from the discussions and information sharing may indicate to them that they cannot be trusted within the family system. They are not allowed to be privy to important news and information because of their limited position and childhood status, rendering them not sufficiently trustworthy to be party to the conversations. This can in turn lead them to conceptualise that they are not worthy of being included, that because of their minor status they should be excluded from something that will have a severe impact on their world. Within the confines of this adult secret, children's imaginations are likely to run riot and cause mayhem for them. Children, particularly younger ones, can misinterpret what they are observing and deduce wrongly that whatever has happened within their family has been caused by their behaviour. This magical thinking is not uncommon and the literature is peppered with examples of where children have created their own, hugely inaccurate, understandings about what has happened (Dunning 2006).

Summary

Communication is an essential part of everyday life and a necessary component of all practitioners' work. In this chapter, different forms of communication have been discussed with emphasis on communicating with children when a parent is at the end of life. Consideration has been given to the differing forms of communication and how these can be incorporated into practice. Where children gather their information about dying and death can influence their understanding and help or hinder the meaning-making process. These different sources include:

- their parents
- professionals
- the media
- books.

The rhetorical question, 'What do you communicate when you do not communicate?' was posed. When children are not included in discussions about their parent's illness, they are being given subconscious messages about the situation. How they interpret these messages will have a significant bearing on how they try to begin to make some meaning of what is occurring. These interpretations are likely to be inaccurate and therefore have the potential to cause the children more anguish than is necessary.

The chapter has considered how important communication is when working with children who are experiencing the death of a parent. The following chapter will begin to explore some of the barriers that are erected when adults contemplate talking to children about dying and death. Barriers that are imposed by parents are discussed along with those erected by professionals in their work. The chapter will then explore ways to develop confidence when working with this population of children.

Chapter 3

Negotiating Conversations
Barriers and Hurdles

The previous chapter began to explore how crucial communication and information sharing are for supporting children's understanding of family life when a parent is terminally ill. Being in a position where they can make informed choices about how much information they feel is necessary for them is important in helping them begin to navigate the alien landscape which they have been forced to enter. Receiving age-appropriate information is, for many children, their comfort blanket. It is something that they can hold onto and from which they receive solace. Importantly, it provides tangible reference points along the route of terminal illness.

The age and developmental level of children significantly determine how their understanding of what is occurring within the family develops and how they are able to process the information that is being given. How children make sense of what is happening and, through this, how they begin to try to make meaning from the situation is crucial in helping them to manage the situation both during the illness and into the bereavement period. This chapter will begin by exploring how children attempt to make some meaning from what is happening. It will then look at barriers that are often erected by parents and professionals alike. Crucially these barriers, whether used consciously or not, can have significant detrimental consequences with regards to how children attempt to make sense of what is occurring and in turn how they manage or, in many cases, fail to manage the situation. The chapter will conclude with practical suggestions to help develop practitioners' skills when communicating with children.

Making sense of the senseless

When a parent is terminally ill, the children will be aware that there are huge changes within their family. No matter how well the adults around them try to pretend that everything is well and to carry on as normal, the children will inevitably begin to recognise that family life is different. Some changes may be more dramatic than others; changes to the parent's health will be a likely indicator. The physical appearance of the parent may alter as the symptoms become more prevalent and the treatment more invasive. Observing dramatic weight loss or gain will alert the children to some differences as will the medical regimes involved in treatment and care. 'Why has Mum got so many hospital appointments?' is a probable observation and a question that deserves an honest answer.

Trying to make sense and meaning from what is happening when a parent is at the end of life is a significant challenge for children. All aspects of family life have the potential to be altered in some way with the onset of terminal illness. Roles within the family are likely to alter along with routines and boundaries. The rhythm of life is disrupted and all that was known and familiar thrown into chaos and confusion.

If the ill parent previously worked and is now unable to, the children will observe this; furthermore, the well parent may have been forced to give up employment in order to care for the ill partner. Again these changes will be indicators to the children that something within their family is amiss. The protective shield is ineffective when such a crisis is being played out in the family and, as I suggested in Chapter 2, the children will draw their own conclusions about what is happening if they are not allowed to be privy to the truth. Knowing what is happening and being involved gives children some control over the situation and helps them to understand more effectively and easily what is occurring. The role of communication, therefore, cannot be underestimated. Being involved in age-appropriate and honest information is probably the resource that will offer most resilience in coping with the unfolding family crisis.

Being able to begin to make some meaning from all that is occurring is important and yet can be obstructed by many factors. As the book attests, information sharing and appropriate language are the bedrock in facilitating this. Moreover, the process of meaning making is helped or hindered by the extent to which family life is disrupted during the terminal stage of the illness. The construct of the family is likely to take on a new identity where the illness becomes the hub of family life. Everything begins to be centred around the treatment and care of the patient. Any spontaneity that the family had previously enjoyed is replaced with medical regimes and hospital appointments. These changes inadvertently disrupt the children's previously known lives and invariably cause them to question their identity and that of their family and the wider community.

The loss of the 'mummy' or 'daddy' role

How children are parented is likely to be affected by the changes within the family. This can have dramatic effects on the children's sense of identity and security. The age of the children will influence how they cope with this. Younger children may struggle to comprehend the changes in how they are parented. The 'mummy role' or 'daddy role' could have seen huge changes and this may have a significant impact on how children internalise what is happening and, as a consequence, how they externalise their behaviour.

Vignette

Sally, the six-year-old whom we met in Chapter 2, becomes a regular visitor on the ward at the specialist palliative care unit. During one of her visits she is invited by the social worker to spend some time in the Activity Room to do some painting. Sally plays for 30 minutes with the social worker and is amicable and engaging. When she returns to the ward she becomes agitated and starts kicking and screaming. Sally's mother watches this episode from her bed and is unable to intervene or comfort her. The social worker tries to manage the situation and placate Sally.

Observations of the vignette

Within this situation the social worker is required to act in loco parentis in attempting to manage Sally's behaviour. Sally's mother is physically there, observing what is happening, but she is unable to take an active role in intervening. This incident with Sally highlights three interrelated observations:

- Sally's behaviour is a manifestation of her anger at the situation. She does not have the vocabulary, means or opportunity to express herself verbally and consequently is forced to find an alternative outlet to express her feelings.

- What messages are being transmitted to Sally as a result of this incident? Mummy no longer does the things that she used to do: 'Now when I am naughty other people take over Mummy's role and try to do what Mummy would have done.'

- What feelings are engendered in Sally's mother as she witnesses this incident and is powerless to parent her as she would have done previously?

For Sally and her mother there is a loss of prescribed familial roles. A fundamental aspect to this for Sally is the limited communication she has been involved in and the sketchy information she has been given. Within such a situation, Sally's ability to begin to make any sense of what is happening is therefore compromised.

Children's interpretations of such incidents are likely to be confused. These changes represent a further transition that the children are required to negotiate. Physical changes are occurring, the parent no longer parents as they did previously and this is accompanied by emotional changes that affect identity, a sense of family cohesion and belonging. This then compounds their ongoing struggle to comprehend all the changes that are occurring within the family.

Older children are also likely to experience the impact of changes within familial roles. Within this they too will need to find ways to express their emotions, especially if communication channels are prohibited, and often in older children these ways are manifested through risk-taking and challenging behaviours. Through these behaviours, children attempt to take some control of the situation, but also the physical pain that sometimes results from these behaviours means that the emotional pain can be briefly blocked. A further transition for older children is that they may be required to take on roles and responsibilities that they would not typically be expected to do. This may include caring for younger siblings or being more involved in household jobs (Lewis 1990).

The children's relationship with the well parent

The vignette with Sally highlighted difficulties she experienced in terms of her relationship with her mother who was the patient. However, relationships with well parents can also be compromised when terminal illness is in the family. Frequently the well parents are so entwined with the illness, caring for their partner and contemplating the future that they have neither the time nor emotional capacity to meet their children's needs. This was noted by Saldinger *et al.* (2004a) who suggested that, just at the time when the children need most support, their intimates are not available because of the pressures and worries of the illness. Christ, Siegel and Sperber (1994) found that often the relationships between adolescents and their well parents were such that the adults needed emotional and practical support leading to conflict, remoteness and even role reversal.

The roles that were previously assigned to the well parents may well have been lost in the tragedy that has occurred in their lives. As a consequence, they are unable to attend to some of the functions they previously performed – for example, transporting the children to social activities or providing support with school work. These losses add to the children's increasing recognition that family life is in a state of flux where they have little control over events.

No matter what the age of the children, the physical, emotional and psychological unavailability of one or both parents can have a severe impact on their understanding of what is happening and how they begin to try to make some sense of their lives. The main priority for well parents is likely to be their partner and the children's needs may be overshadowed by the enormity of what is happening within the relationship. If the well parents struggle to balance the emotional and physical demands of caring for their partner with the parenting role, opportunities to communicate may become less prevalent or indeed totally subsumed under the weight of worry and anxiety of caring for a dying partner. It is therefore important that professionals working with the family regularly assess how open the communication channels are. Within this assessment, consideration needs to be given to the appropriate time for intervention. Exploring with the well and ill parents their perspectives about talking with the children is helpful in determining whether their silence is 'purposefully planned' or 'deliberately managed'. If it is the latter, and the parents have decided that it is in the best interest of their children not to talk to them about what is happening, the worker should begin gently to explore their reasoning. Ways of working with such resistance will be explored later in this chapter.

Facing the news that the illness is terminal

Being given the news that an illness is terminal and that the only viable treatment available is palliative in nature is a hugely traumatic body blow for any patient. While ever-curative treatment is an option, there is some small hope that the medical establishment can treat the illness and that the patient will return to better health. The metaphor of a battle is frequently used to denote this (DasGupta, Irvine and Spiegel 2009) – for example, 'She is fighting cancer', 'With the right treatment this can be beaten' and 'He has lost his battle'. However, once this 'battle' has been lost and a terminal stage entered, so too has the lingering hope that was associated with it been lost.

The point when the treatment loses its curative status and becomes palliative is the time when difficult decisions need to be made about talking with the children. Even if the children are aware and informed that the parent is ill, the disclosure of the change in status is very difficult. Being in the position of having to tell your children that you are dying is heart-wrenchingly difficult (MacPherson 2005) and something that no one wants to contemplate. It is difficult to imagine a more difficult journey for any family, especially when there appears to be no alternative routes available.

The news that the illness has become terminal is devastating for all the family. With the news comes the disruption to all plans, hopes and dreams for the future. The mapped-out life of the family comes to a violent, shuddering halt where everything needs to be re-evaluated. For the patient there are a number of sociological and emotional changes that accompany the news. Questions about their role within the family are likely to be raised including issues regarding the here and now but also about the future. Philosophical and practical thoughts about their continuing presence within the family life, whether and how they will be remembered and what legacy they will leave are not unusual. Equally, the parents are likely to reflect on how they have parented their children and who can take over such a role. Will the surviving parent recognise and understand the idiosyncratic ways that help form each child's identity and personality? Will they be able to provide the same level of nurturing care and support and travel with the children in the same direction? These and a plethora of other questions are likely to seep into the parents' conscious thoughts as they digest the news that nothing more can be done to help them. These questions are difficult enough to contemplate for parents who are in a stable relationship but, for ill parents who are not in a relationship, they are likely to be magnified considerably and this is something that professionals need to be cognisant of when working with families. In these situations, the welfare of the children needs to become a priority and careful planning for their futures should be a primary concern.

A report in *The Daily Telegraph* (2010) described how a mother who, aware that she was dying from breast cancer, wrote a list, for her husband, of over one hundred things he should do to help raise their two young sons. Part of the article, entitled 'Mother knows best: The instructions', lists her hopes and aspirations for the boys. A legacy to her children was her continued parenting via her husband.

This philosophical thinking is not only the preserve of the ill parent. The well parents are also likely to be swamped with questions, thoughts and ideas about the present situation and the future. They too need to assimilate the information and begin to process what is going to happen. Some couples formulate plans together in preparation for when the ill parent dies and these include deciding how the children will be parented in the future and how the legacies of the dead parent will be remembered and maintained. In especially insightful families, the children are also included in these discussions and permitted to play an active role in the planning of their future.

Barriers to parents communicating with their children

In the midst of the trauma of receiving the news that the illness has become terminal, there is a need to think about whether and how this information is to be conveyed to the children. It is generally assumed that the parents are the most appropriate people to communicate such news to their children. After all, they know the children best and how the family generally communicates; they have the 'family scripts' to hand. Nevertheless, being forced into the position of having to contemplate telling your children that you are dying is one of the hardest conversations a parent will ever have to face.

To tell or not to tell

Different theories as to why parents do not include their children in information sharing about the terminal status of the illness can be speculated on. In many examples, their reasoning is commendable because they are trying to protect their children from what they perceive to be unnecessary pain and anguish; however, this protective behaviour has a number of ramifications. The non-inclusion can act as a signal to the children that they are living in the midst of a family secret that they are not permitted to be part of. However, as discussed earlier, young family members are invariably aware that something serious is occurring within their family and, if a conspiracy of silence is maintained, their imaginative minds will be likely to run riot. Attempting to protect children from the painful news that a parent is dying can therefore be a false economy. Likewise, some parents believe that the children are too young to understand and therefore do not need to be included in what is happening; the logic here being that, if they do not know what is happening, they will not worry. However, research suggests that children as young as three years old have a limited understanding of what is happening in families when a parent has a terminal illness (Christ and Christ 2006).

The barrier to communicating with children is sometimes erected because the parents do not know what to say or how to say it. How do parents find the words to tell their children? For some parents, if they do not verbalise what is happening and do not consciously contemplate the enormity of the situation, they can manage to avoid having to envisage the reality of their lives. Adopting the earlier analogy of a battle, telling the children is almost like the final act of capitulation to the battle that everyone hoped could be won. Presenting the children with the information is the final surrender and the sign that all hope has been lost. Chapter 2 highlighted that finding the right time to have such conversations is often peppered with obstacles and that there is the mistaken belief that putting off the inevitable will be less painful and stressful for all concerned. The role of professionals involved with the family is important here, especially in exploring with the parents what they have already shared with the children, how much they think the children know and their plans for talking with the children about the situation now. However, research would suggest that often professionals working with families do not provide support or guidance to parents about how to communicate with their children (Elmberger, Bolund and Lutzen 2005; Turner *et al.* 2005). This, as we shall see in the next section, is often because the professionals are unsure what to say and do not feel that they have the appropriate tools in their 'bag of work' to facilitate the conversations.

The imposed silence by adults can not only create extreme fear and uncertainty but also develop a culture of mistrust. Children typically perceive the relationship with their parents to be built on trust, which in turn creates a sense of security and belonging. When the trust has been dented, it is often difficult to undertake reparation and rebuild those feelings. Therefore, neglecting to be honest with children can weaken their trust in the surviving parent (Siegel *et al.* 1990) and other significant adults.

The family's communication culture

Different factors that might underpin the parents' rationale for not including their children in conversations about the illness include the family's history of communication styles. If the family has previously engaged in a form of closed communication, the burden of living with the knowledge that one of the parents is terminally ill is likely to compound their established pattern of communication. The family's culture has a bearing on communication styles, the dominant embedded practice typically being prevalent at times of crisis. Writing specifically with families where a parent has cancer, Lewandowski (1996) observed that:

> Many families in which a parent has cancer seem to function under an implicit 'don't ask, don't tell' communication system. In these cases the children and adolescents are unlikely to be asked directly about their thoughts, worries and feelings and are unlikely to feel free to volunteer this information. (p.519)

Research by MacPherson (2005) found that not sharing information and not communicating with children about the terminal illness was directly related to the parents' ability to talk together about the illness.

The dying parent influenced the decision about whether the children were informed about the prognosis and the well parent followed this example.

The community's communication culture

The parents' decision whether or not to discuss the situation with the children may also be influenced by the ideologies of society, along with the opinions and views of family and friends. The dominant view held by society remains such that children do not need to be included in an attempt to protect them and maintain their innocence. However, when the rights of children are recognised and taken into consideration, this paternalistic standpoint has to be questioned. The prevailing consensus is that, in the majority of situations, children should be included and that shielding them from what is happening is deleterious both in the short and longer term. Family and friends may also contribute to the discussions and offer well-intentioned advice relating to the non inclusion of the children. These opinions, while probably offered in the most sincere and well-meaning ways, can be unhelpful and obstructive in the way the parents' decision-making process about informing the children is structured.

Professionals have a significant role here in first exploring with the parents and then facilitating the conversations to go ahead. These initial enquiries can be very gentle in nature to ascertain whether the children have been told anything and how much they know. This can then be followed up with a discussion outlining the benefits of telling the children and the potential implications of not informing them. Through these discussions, the professional can begin to make an assessment of the parents' capacity, ability and desire to talk with their children about what is happening.

It's not denial, it is just getting on with it

There are occasions when parents may appear to be avoiding talking about the situation and could therefore be assessed as being in denial. However, the reality might be that they have spoken to the children, they have been included in discussions and now the family as a unit is getting on with 'business as usual'. This is not the same as situations where families refuse to acknowledge the impending death and where there remains an adamantly silenced barrier that prevents the children from being included. Where families are 'getting on with it', there is generally the acknowledgement that family members can broach the subject when required but are also permitted to cope in a proactive way with living with dying.

The subtle use of language

Parents will sometimes employ subtle communication styles where the content is equally unhelpful – for example, saying to the children: 'Daddy is poorly but you don't want to know about that at the moment, do you?' or 'Mummy doesn't want you to be upset and I think talking about her being poorly will make you sad; you don't want to upset Mummy, do you?' The negative, inverse undertones in such conversations send very powerful messages to the children about the situation. These examples suggest that clearly the language used is so powerful in communicating with children. Parents who have adopted this language could assure professionals that they have spoken to their children and they, the children, have decided that they do not want any more information at the moment. However, in reality, while it is true that the parents have spoken to their children, their discourse is such that it is prohibitive. Being aware that it is not always *what* is said but rather *how* it is said is important when assessing families' communication. However, professionals can be equally guilty of adopting subtle language that is obstructive in facilitating opportunities for meaningful conversations.

Cultural difference in communication

Consideration needs to be given to the families' cultural and religious beliefs. The practices of different ethnic minority communities may be very different from the dominant British belief system. Therefore, what may be considered as a barrier to communicating with children could be part of the cultural heritage. It is therefore important that professionals who are involved with the families ascertain some awareness of the beliefs and wishes and never make assumptions about their practices.

The value for children of talking with non-familial people

The importance and relevance of parents' communicating with their children should not be underestimated; however, there are also times when the children need non-familial people to converse with (Fearnley 2010). Having the opportunity to talk with a professional and to gain the specialist's view could present children with a more comprehensive account of what is currently occurring in their family and help solidify their narratives, but it could also act to reinforce and substantiate their parents' conversations. Moreover, being able to talk to someone who understands what is happening but who is emotionally detached may open up conversation opportunities that would not be available between parent and child.

Just as parents sometimes try to protect their children from the harsh realities of living with a terminal illness, the reverse is also often acted out. Children will invoke a self-imposed silence to help protect their parents. They may opt not to talk to their parents so as not to burden them with additional worries or problems, especially when they can see the parents are struggling to cope with their own emotions. A prolonged self-imposed silence is likely to be unhelpful and, therefore, having the opportunity to talk to a professional can be a positive experience for children of all ages. Here they can explore their feelings in a safe environment and express how they are feeling without fear of causing their parents any upset or worries.

Parents will have many different reasons for not communicating with their children the news that they are terminally ill. The fear of upsetting the children or causing them confusion and anxiety are often cited. While these reasons are truly valid at one level, at another this protective behaviour can be seen as being damaging and unhelpful. Parents are generally working within what they believe to be the best interests of their children, and the barriers are a genuine response to the most difficult of situations. However, as the following section illustrates, professionals too will erect communication barriers when working with children whose parents are dying.

Barriers to professionals communicating with this population of children

In our professional lives, communication is tightly entwined with all our practice and can be seen as the major resource in helping us to fulfil our daily tasks; in fact, without the ability to communicate, we would be quite inefficient in our roles! No matter which profession a person belongs to, some conversations will be less threatening, more eagerly anticipated and more easily achieved than others. Imparting good news is always much easier than having to face the 'bad news' interview; however, Buckman (1992) encouragingly tells the reader that such interviews do become easier with practice. Being asked to work with children whose parents are terminally ill generally means that some elements of the bad news interview are likely to be prevalent. If the remit of your job is to work directly with children, the prospect of undertaking the task of talking with them may be a little less daunting. Nevertheless, these conversations can still create some anxieties and worries. I recall driving to interview two children for my doctoral research. They had been bereaved of their father and I felt anxious about the meeting; the only rationale I could assign to this feeling related to the subject matter I was about to discuss. I remember vocally reprimanding myself as I drove to their house – 'How ridiculous you are being' and 'Practice what you preach'; however, a small flicker of anxiety remained until I had been welcomed into the family home.

The following section presents some of the typical barriers that are erected by professionals when faced with the task of talking to children about parental terminal illness. Some of the barriers may be more salient for some professionals than others; however, they all contribute to the exclusion of children from conversations that are both relevant and important.

Death and dying: the great taboo

The first of these is the dominant cultural view whereby talking about dying and death remains taboo for many in modern Britain. Whether death is taboo continues to be debated by academics. Some would argue that rather than death being a forbidden topic, it is more that it is hidden from ordinary life (Reith and Payne 2009). However, it has been suggested that possibly the primary people in society who are responsible for maintaining this taboo are those in the medical profession (Walter 1991). Recent research would certainly suggest that doctors, particularly general practitioners (GPs), continue to have difficulties talking about dying and death with their patients. In a pilot study undertaken by the organisation Dying Matters, 60 per cent of the GPs taking part stated that they were not confident initiating conversations about dying. However, following training, 86 per cent rated themselves post-pilot as 'confident' (Lakhani 2011). If the professionals working with dying patients do not feel confident talking about dying and death, the children of these patients will face a double jeopardy. The reluctance of the professionals will only increase the view that this is a subject that should be avoided at all costs; after all, if the GP does not talk about it, how can we? The elephant remains obstinately in the room.

Let's protect the children

Professionals try to alleviate distress and to make the situation better, particularly when they are aware that the service user is distressed (Heaven and Maguire 2005). Reasons for professionals not communicating with children and not engaging them in discussions include the fear of upsetting them and making the situation worse. Coupled with these reasons are the innate feelings of wanting to protect them and the belief that they are 'better off not knowing'. The fear of upsetting children and the cognition that it is better for them not to know what is happening are paternalistic views about children and childhood. Jones (2009) argues that adults' attitudes towards childhood exclude and silence children and this can be exemplified in professionals' reluctance to talk to children about dying and death.

However, here lies an ethical dilemma that professionals are likely to encounter in their practice. The notion of adopting the mantra 'communication, communication, communication' has blurred boundaries. It would be incorrect and morally wrong to suggest that in all circumstances children should be given detailed information about their parent's illness and the likelihood of their death. A caveat here is about knowing the child, the family's culture and background circumstances. However, as has already been discussed in Chapter 1, the general consensus is that it is preferable that children are included in conversations about their parent's illness (Christ 2000a; Christ and Christ 2006; Rauch *et al.* 2002; Thastum *et al.* 2008) and have the opportunity to choose the extent of this inclusion. Moreover, Beale *et al.* (2004) highlighted that anxiety in children is increased when information is available but no opportunities are provided to allow them to explore what has been said. It is also important here to recognise the needs and wishes of the children. The Children Act 1989 emphasises the rights of children in relation to having their wishes and feelings heard (Seden 2006) and a number of the articles in the United Nations Convention on the Rights of the Child (United Nations 1989) are salient to this population of children.

Professionals working in health and social care have spoken of their concerns of 'making it worse' if they talk to children about their parent's illness. However, one professional whose role was to work with children of terminally ill patients observed that the worst had actually happened and no amount of 'protecting' the children could make it any worse (Fearnley 2010).

Let's protect ourselves

While some professionals believe that they are protecting children from the harsh realities of their current lived experience, others may consciously, or subconsciously, erect barriers in order to protect themselves. If unresolved issues of personal grief are present or workers feels uncomfortable contemplating dying and death, it is likely that they will shield their own feelings by avoiding any talk with children about their issues. Discussing issues that are emotionally saturated can engender a strong sense of anxiety and as a result defence mechanisms come into play to keep such feelings at a safe distance. It could be argued that professionals who advertently, or inadvertently, adopt the notion that they are likely to upset children by talking with them, or that they are better off not knowing about what is happening in their families, are displacing their own beliefs and attitudes on to the children.

Not knowing what to say and feeling that the appropriate words are not readily available can be a huge block to effective communication and impinge on the quality of work offered to children. If workers have such feelings, they may 'protect' themselves in order not to look incompetent or so that their perceived weaknesses do not have to be confronted. There is also the concern that the worker will be 'starting something' they cannot finish. The anxiety here is that they will not have the necessary skills or knowledge to follow the children in their discussions and will be left feeling that they are unable to complete what they started. This may arise because they are unsure of what information to share with the children; they may not have the necessary knowledge about the illness trajectory and symptoms or they may feel that the children will want to explore inevitably 'difficult' questions about the parent's death.

Engrained in the psyche of professionals is the notion that if difficult questions are asked they require difficult answers. This has the potential to create anxieties, which in turn blocks opportunities to engage in conversations. However, not having all the answers is not a failure and is not a sign of incompetence. Being able to say to a child, 'Do you know, I don't know the answer to that' can be very empowering, and an even more productive reply is when you suggest endeavouring to find the answers together. However, recognising that within this work there will be times when there are simply no answers to be given is important. Therefore, the need to have solutions is not always necessary – using the resource of listening and being alongside the children as they explore their feelings, worries and fears can be as helpful and supportive as any amount of advice giving and talking.

For some professionals, the barrier is a result of the belief that it is not part of their job to work with children. A specialist nurse told me, during my research, that 'I work with adults.' The sad reflection is that this is too often the situation. Professional roles are tightly boundaried and, consequently, this nurse's role was with the adult patients, leaving little or no scope for working holistically with the families.

Being confident and feeling at ease discussing dying and death is therefore important in helping professionals become better equipped to communicate with children about their parent's terminal illness and likely death. Whether the barriers are erected to protect the workers from their own sadness and pain or are there as a result of not feeling capable of engaging with the children, supportive work needs to be undertaken to help address the issues and to develop skills. Exploring these issues with a trusted colleague or friend, or taking them to supervision, are ways forward to enable workers to process their thoughts and feelings and to develop strategies for more effective practice.

Professional jargon

A barrier that is often employed during conversations is the use of jargon. Employing professional jargon and acronyms gives a clear message that the content of the discussion is situated within the domain of professionals and not easily accessible by service users. Jargon is often the common discourse employed between colleagues and it is therefore easy to slip into such language when working with children. The skilled communicator will effectively move from 'professional speak' to a more child-friendly approach when required. However, the less competent workers may use this 'safe' language to provide a potent mask to hide behind. This 'professional mask' is an effective tool for protecting workers and allows them to hide behind a professional façade. Writing some 40 years ago, Kavanaugh (1972) described how doctors, nurses, clergymen and funeral directors put on different masks to help move them one step away from dying and death. He suggests that some of these masks are cruel and can be actually harmful to patients and their families. Almost half a century later, and despite the numerous advancements in medical and social care, the same masks appear to be thriving in some areas.

Time: the great barrier

The barriers that are erected by professionals often have compelling arguments attached as to why the communication exchange cannot be developed. Professionals from all disciplines are currently drowning under the pressure of work. Time is at a premium and with ever-increasing caseloads to manage along with the upsurge in paperwork and record keeping, opportunities to spend time undertaking face-to-face work with service users is decreasing. This 'time poor' environment is frequently used as a reason for not initiating conversations with children. Within my research (Fearnley 2010), a participant described personal observations of colleagues who were anxious that talking with children would 'take too much time'. It cannot be denied that such conversations are likely to take time and cannot be undertaken glibly in passing. However, the benefits of investing that time are likely to be invaluable for the children, in the short term before their parent's death, into the bereavement period and beyond into their adult lives.

Whatever form the communication barrier takes, it assists the worker to become 'communicatively paralysed' and prevents meaningful, helpful interactions from taking place. Communicating with children about their current situation is not only beneficial to them during the terminal period of their parent's life but also into their bereavement. Dunning (2006) demonstrated this when she wrote 'a child who is well prepared for the death, who knows what will happen, and who understands what has happened is in a good position to begin the mourning process' (p.500).

When there are complex and complicated barriers (perceived or real) to communication

Working with terminal illness entails professionals encountering families from all socio-economic backgrounds, cultures and diversities. Families that do not fit the stereotypical representation could present practitioners with different and 'difficult' challenges and create additional barriers to their communication. The scope of this book will not permit these issues to be comprehensively addressed; however, some acknowledgement and recognition of them needs to be made.

Single parents

When working with single parents there could be different communication demands placed on the worker that would not be encountered when working with two-parent families. Different issues are likely to be presented in relation to the care of the children both during the terminal stage and following the death. The parents are likely to share similar anxieties, about communicating with their children, as other parents but they are also potentially experiencing additional concerns. Some of these may originate from worries about issues of residency, where the children will live, whether the person will offer the same standard of parenting efficacy, whether siblings will be separated and whether the children will settle into this new environment. Practitioners working with single-parent families need to be cognisant of these dilemmas and worries and be proactive in exploring them with the parent but also with the children. The children are quite probably thinking through these issues and the issues could be compounding their ability to cope with the situation. The children will potentially have many questions about their future that will need to be addressed. Practitioners need to be vigilant to these thoughts and feelings, and be prepared to explore them when working with the children. Chapter 5 explores practical ways of working with children that will assist in this process.

Children with additional needs

When children have a disability, family members are often reluctant to talk with them about the parent's ill health (Barnes *et al.* 1998). Moreover, there could equally be hesitance on the part of professionals working with the family. A barrier here could be uncertainty about how to communicate and about the amount the children can comprehend. Factors that the practitioners need to consider, before embarking on any work with children with disabilities, include ascertaining what the disability is, the severity of it and how it affects the children's ability to communicate. With this information, steps can then be taken to ensure that appropriate forms of communication are deployed. Chapter 5 offers practical ways of communicating with children, and these can be adapted when working with children who have a disability. Again the parents are likely to have additional worries and concerns pertaining to the care of their children as their own health deteriorates and following their death. Barnes *et al.* (1998) highlight this when they describe how young people with disabilities have heightened dependence on their caregivers that is compromised when the caregiver is terminally ill. Therefore, this is an important concern that practitioners need to approach sensitively when talking with the parents. Being proactive to put in place plans for the care of the children is particularly salient in these situations. It is important here that the plans are completed in partnership with the children and that they are aware of them.

Black and ethnic minority families

Working with families who do not share the same cultural heritage as the practitioner can present challenges in relation to knowing what is permissible to discuss and what is culturally insensitive. Throughout the book, I have alluded to the individual and unique way families begin to cope with terminal illness. There is no 'one size fits all' and each case needs to be approached on its individual merit. Within this, practitioners need to take into consideration the family culture of communication and how the family functions as a unit. However, as Smaje and Field (1997) describe, 'there is a widespread feeling in the British palliative care community that people from minority ethnic populations are under represented among the users of services for the dying' (p.142). If this situation remains, there are potential ramifications for practitioner confidence in communicating with families and especially children from ethnic backgrounds. Respecting the cultural norms and practices is important while balancing the needs of the children. In some circumstances, the children may be more fluent in English than their parents and may act as interpreters. This can cause ethical dilemmas – for example, should children be given the responsibility of passing on information to their parents about their health and the illness trajectory? Moreover, the practitioner needs to know how much information the children have about the illness and how much, within their culture, they are permitted to know. Being aware therefore of customs and traditions is important before engaging in any conversations with children. In these situations, it is important to seek advice from colleagues and other sources to ensure that respectful practice is undertaken. Being open and honest with the family and saying, 'I'm not familiar with how your culture deals with this. Can you help me?' is a positive starting point.

Developing skills in communicating with this population of children

To date the chapter has considered some of the barriers parents and professionals experience when confronted with having to talk to children about parental terminal illness. The final part of the chapter will look towards practical ways professionals can begin to develop their communication skills with this population of children. It is important here to recognise that these children have a right to be communicated with and that moreover they need to be included in what appears to be very difficult conversations.

Heaven and Maguire (2005), writing specifically about palliative care professionals' communication skills, suggest that 'the key to improving communication is to understand how and why it breaks down. Only then can health professionals begin to develop more effective communication behaviours' (p.15). Heaven and Maguire's work focuses predominantly on communication between nursing and medical staff and patients and has many parallels with the ideas being proposed in this book. Understanding why communication breaks down and developing skills to help prevent this breakdown are key to helping professionals become more confident and competent communicators with children.

An important part of developing communication skills to help children whose parents are dying is having the reflexive self-awareness to recognise and acknowledge that, when embarking on such communication exchanges, feelings of confidence and competence may be challenged. Because communication is seen as the bedrock of all encounters with service users, in whatever situation, professionals sometimes feel that to admit that they are not confident beginning work with these children is a sign of incompetence or weakness. This can then act as a serious barrier to effective work. Therefore, spending time reflecting on and assessing where you think your strengths in communicating lie, and where you believe that there might be underdeveloped strengths, is a positive starting point.

Exercise

Being comfortable using the words 'dying', 'dead' and 'bereavement' is really important if we are going to communicate successfully with children about their parent's terminal illness. Do you have a fear about talking and thinking about the subject? Would you rather avoid it and consciously take steps not to think about it? Is it the elephant in your room?

If you recognise that you have difficulties using this language, reflect why this is the case. What do the barriers look like, where have they come from and who can begin to help break them down? Try practising using them with colleagues and trusted friends. This will help you to prepare for the times when you are working with children, to remove some of the uncomfortable feelings associated with the words and to feel more confident in what you say.

Confronting these feelings and exploring where they have originated from can be painful, test our emotions and push our secure boundaries to the limit. However, if we are prepared to explore and recognise them, we can then begin to understand our feelings and through this become more effective in undertaking those 'difficult' conversations with children. Our own unresolved issues of grief are likely to play a significant part in contributing to these feelings and barriers. Being forced, in a professional capacity, to think about childhood bereavement can be a powerful tool for activating emotions and memories that are best left dormant in the depths of unconsciousness. Confronting such feelings is not easy and needs to be undertaken carefully and with support; however, it is imperative that this is achieved in order to be effective when communicating with children whose parents are at the end of life. As we have seen, being comfortable and at ease with any subject matter is crucial in enabling positive and meaningful interactions with service users and in developing professional working relationships that are built on trust and understanding.

An important question concerns the commonly held subjective notion that conversations in these circumstances are difficult. Is there some form of transference occurring, are the conversations truly difficult for the children, is it our perceptions that they are difficult for them or is it our thoughts and anxieties that are telling us that they are difficult for the children? In such situations who are we trying to protect, the children or ourselves? Children typically have a much more resilient and sophisticated system for coping than adults give them credit for. They can be told anything – it is how it is told and the support that is available following the telling that are the crucial factors here. Moreover, if children ask questions about what is happening, they have the right to accurate answers.

Vignette

Lucy, a recently qualified social worker, now working in a family support team, has been allocated Michael, a nine-year-old whose father has heart disease. The referral is for help with Michael's behaviour, which has deteriorated recently. Having been allocated Michael, Lucy takes the case to supervision. She tentatively tells her manager that she does not know how to work with Michael, what to say to him and how she can offer any support. During supervision, Lucy's manager suggests that she reflects on the communication skills she has brought into the team. The manager asks Lucy to rate her overall competence when communicating with service users. Lucy is informed that the scale is where 0 equals very limited and poor communication skills and 10 equals highly developed communication skills. She is then asked to repeat the exercise but this time focusing on communicating with children when a parent is at the end of life. The manager explores with Lucy the different scores she has allocated herself and asks her what she thinks she would need to do to move up the second scale. The manager suggests that she should again think about the skills she has brought to the team and then consider which of these are transferable into the specific situation of working with Michael. Within the exercise, Lucy's two scores differed. When thinking about her overall competence she rated herself at 7, but when she moved to the second half of the exercise she rated herself at 3. She justified these differing scores to her manager by saying that she felt quite comfortable talking generally to service users but thought that initiating conversations with children like Michael would be more difficult. She felt that it would be hard to begin the conversation and wondered how she could approach the subject of Michael's father's illness. She questioned whether she might be giving him information that he was not aware of and how this would be accepted by both Michael and his father. She doubted that it was her role to give 'new' information to Michael and was apprehensive that this would lead to difficult conversations and problems. Her manager encouraged her to think about her experiences when on placement and when she had volunteered as a support worker at an after-school activity centre. Through this, Lucy began to recognise that she had some skills that could be transferred when working with Michael.

Exercise

Reflect on how you communicate generally within your practice and then undertake the task set by Lucy's manager. Think about the skills that you have, and rate yourself on how effective you believe you are (0 = very poor, 10 = excellent). Now think more specifically about how you would rate your communication skills when communicating with children who are experiencing the death of a parent. Again use the scale 0 to 10. Then ask yourself the following questions:

- Are both scores similar or are there marked differences between the two?

- How could I move up the second scale in order to improve my rating of my communication skills with children?

- What transferable skills do I have that would help with this?

- What else do I need to do to help develop my communication skills with children whose parents are dying?

If possible, repeat this exercise with a trusted colleague who will give open and honest feedback.

Vignette

Having completed the exercises set by her manager, Lucy reflected on the skills she currently had. She was then able to begin to explore which parts of the skills mix she felt were underdeveloped and would benefit from some nurturing. She recognised that a skill that had been encouraged while on placement had been the ways she had developed introductory written material to children. Drawing on her creative skills, she had developed some imaginative introductory letters that were sent to the children referred to the centre where she was on final placement. She reflected on how initially these letters had been stilted and adult orientated, but as the placement progressed she had been able to hone her skills in order to make them more child friendly. She also recalled how she had received some very positive feedback from the service users about her initial approach and ability to engage children. She then thought about her apprehensions about starting conversations with Michael and wondered whether this was because she struggled to use the words 'dying', 'cancer' and 'terminal'. She had not experienced any deaths in her young life and had never attended a funeral. Moreover, her family never discussed death, always opting to change the subject rapidly if the topic was mentioned. She recognised that she could not draw on personal experience to help her begin to plan her work with Michael.

Observations on the vignette

Developing communication skills with this population of children takes time and practice and, as with all skills, needs to be nurtured. A starting point to doing this could be to explore with colleagues, who have experience of communicating with children, how they undertake such conversations. Asking them what their worries, fears and experiences are may help in creating a baseline. They may be able to offer suggestions about creative ways of engaging in conversations, along with practical ideas for taking the work forward.

Child development books: a cautionary tale

In Chapter 2 child development, in relation to children's understanding of dying and death, was briefly discussed. It is important, when in practice, to have an understanding of child development to help nurture communication skills. Child development books are available that present easily accessible résumés of how children develop and what is typically seen at each age and stage of development. However, a word of caution needs to be offered. These books are generally written within the 'normal' parameters of children's lives and therefore the development being described, along with the ages and stages of the children, will be written with 'typical' child development in mind. The children who are the focus of this book are mostly living in circumstances that are not within the 'normal' parameters of family life. They are likely to have been exposed to stress and upheaval that are unique to the confines of living with a parent who is terminally ill, and to experiences that are outside the expected norm for their developmental stage and that of their family (Dunning 2006). Therefore, their development may have been affected by the circumstances they are living in. It is not unusual for children's behaviour to regress when their parent is dying or for their development to be temporarily arrested. Their ability to process information may be affected along with their capacity to comprehend what they are being told. Consequently, while the child development books suggest that at a certain age children will be able to undertake particular cognitive tasks, this may not be an appropriate expectation of children who are living with a parent who is dying. Intertwined with an understanding of child development theory is the need to be flexible in your communication style. Recognising that it is very different talking to a five-year-old compared with a 17-year-old is an essential component in developing communication skills. Therefore, when considering how communication skills can be developed, this needs to be taken into account.

Jargon and children's understanding

The use of jargon was discussed earlier with particular reference to how, at times, professionals use it as a protective barrier. In relation to children's understanding, it is important to recognise how employing such language has the potential to create misunderstandings. For example, talking to children about chemotherapy without explaining in simple terms what it is, why it is used as a treatment and the possible side effects may cause confusion and fear. Therefore, when thinking about developing communication skills, it is important to consider carefully the language that is being used and adapt it to meet the needs and understanding of the children with whom you are working. However, it is also important to be well prepared and to have planned for the session. Having information to hand will help in building your confidence and assist in communicating with the children. Returning to the chemotherapy example, having some knowledge about why it is being used as a treatment and how it works will help when working with the children. This does not mean that you need immediately to become an 'expert' in the field but to possess some understanding is valuable. The Internet is a good resource to help gather information and assist in your understanding but so too are colleagues or professionals working specifically in oncology. Discussing with them their knowledge and experiences of, for example, using chemotherapy will help in gaining sufficient insight to equip you with a basic understanding. Moreover, there are national support organisations for many of the more prevalent diseases and illnesses. These organisations generally produce written materials that can be used to inform understanding, and these often include those that have been written with the specific intention of use with children (for example, the Motor Neurone Disease Association has produced a workbook for children aged four to ten, *When Someone Close Has MND* (2009)).

Developing 'grass-roots' work

When considering developing communication skills with this population of children, it is valuable to return to what I call 'grass-roots' work. This requires workers really to take a child-centred approach and to de-centre their work to accommodate the needs of the children. This includes focusing on using age-appropriate language and ensuring that there is sufficient time allocated to the session and pacing of the discussions so that the children are not overloaded with information and are able to process what is being said in their own time.

Developing safe boundaries

Creating safe boundaries is part of developing a grass-roots approach. All children thrive when they have routines and boundaries in their lives (Quinton 2006). However, children who are living with the uncertainty and fear of parental terminal illness often experience a loss of previously known boundaries. The daily routines that set the parameters of their lives are shaken because the illness becomes the hub of family life and within this some of the boundaries that had previously been established are eradicated. Sometimes this occurs unwittingly as the enormity of what is occurring is unfolding; at other times parenting styles alter and the children are given more freedom than they previously enjoyed. Losing safe, secure boundaries when it feels as though everything else is falling apart can be difficult to manage. Therefore, establishing boundaries within the working relationship with the children is crucial. Even if the communication exchange is going to be brief and a one-off, it is still important to set boundaries. Whether the session is a short five-minute conversation or a lengthier, structured time, setting in place simple boundaries will be beneficial. A good starting point here is to tell the children from the outset how long you will be seeing them. The use of visual aids such as a clock or egg timer can help the children to relate to the time available to them. This advanced warning helps even small children to know that the session is time limited. Setting time limits is not only beneficial for the children, it also aids workers to manage more effectively the time they have available. Without such boundaries it would be easy to let the session go on for longer than is necessary or helpful to the child. Equally, agreeing that it is permissible to stop the session or move away from the central discussion at any point is good practice in creating a safe environment for the children. This will be returned to again in Chapter 5.

Planning and preparation

Another grass-roots approach that is helpful is to plan before the session how it is going to be managed. If this is the first meeting with a child, how will you introduce yourself? Will you immediately start talking about why you are there and almost rush to get the session over with? This again relates to pacing the sessions and considering carefully the needs of the children and the approach taken. Giving them the opportunity to say why they think you are meeting helps you to make an assessment of what they already know about the situation and also, importantly, gives them a voice early on in the encounter, which in turn helps them feel that what they have to say is valued and important.

Thinking about your approach is helpful, and within this acknowledging your role is important. In part, this is about determining how you see your role and managing professional boundaries. It is about finding the balance between the professional who hides behind the professional mask and being the children's friend, which is inappropriate. A 'friendly professional' would be the ideal position, which means that you remain professional in your role but are also friendly and approachable and demonstrate a genuine interest in the children's lives. However, this view is being oversimplified. The children may not want to engage with you for a raft of reasons. Being forced into an encounter with a professional may trigger feelings of resentment and anger – 'Why do I need to talk to somebody? I know very well what is happening in my family. I just don't need some do-gooder interfering.' Alternatively it may be that having to talk about what is happening and consciously face up to the present and future is too painful at the moment and needs to be revisited later.

Power dynamics

The Anne-Mei (2002), writing about the patient–doctor relationship, suggests that 'the social distance between doctor and patient is often large' (p.21). This, she argues, is because of doctors' perceived positioning in society, their education becoming representative of something that patients look up to. In a similar vein, children will be likely to assign professionals with great authority. After all, you are working with the team who is caring for their parent, and that position is all-powerful! Therefore, being able to abdicate some of that power to the children in a thoughtful and carefully planned way will help readdress the imbalance. This is again about planning and preparing for the work. Thinking through how the work is to be approached and ensuring that opportunities for addressing the power imbalance are incorporated into the session will be helpful.

When planning the work, it may be helpful to try to put yourself in the shoes of the children. If you were in their situation, what would you really want? Would you want a worker who presented as being very uncomfortable in their role, someone who had no confidence and spluttered and fumbled their way through the discussion? Or would you prefer someone who had the ability to put you at ease, who spoke confidently and demonstrated an understanding and empathy?

Team exercise

If you work within a team, request that within a team meeting time is allocated for a group exercise. With a blank sheet of flip-chart paper and sticky notes, ask the team to 'build' their perfect communicator. Things to consider when creating this person include:

- What skills would this person have?

- What would these skills look like?

- Where would these skills have developed from?

Following the 'building' of this communicator, reflect collectively and individually about the core features that have been identified. How could you incorporate some of the features into your practice? If the team is particularly cohesive, it might be possible to develop the exercise so that colleagues highlight who, within the team, enjoys such attributes. However, if you do not work in a team, the exercise can be completed individually.

This exercise would be especially helpful for Lucy because it would help her identify team members whom she could talk to about developing her own communication skills.

Developing listening skills

The emphasis to date has been on engaging with and talking to children. However, the skills needed for listening are also vitally important when developing communication skills. Rosenblatt (2000), writing about the professional's listening skills, suggests that 'an astute listener would do well to pay attention to what is not being said' (p.6). This relates closely to the vignette in Chapter 2 where the social worker was talking with Sally. Here the social worker 'heard' Sally's words, but did not hear the meaning or interpretation of the comments.

Taking time to listen carefully to what is being said and to practise these skills are important components in becoming a more skilled communicator. Silences within sessions can feel particularly uncomfortable and there is an instinctive need to fill the silence with talk. However, sometimes silence allows the reflective process to be undertaken and gives both the children and the worker space to think through the information that is being imparted. Therefore, developing self-awareness where you feel comfortable with silences is important. If within a session there is silence and the urge to re-start the conversation takes hold, simply take a breath and consciously make yourself pause. Ask yourself why there is a silence. Has everything that could possibly have been said on the subject been said? Is there more to be discussed, but does the child need time to think about everything before you can carry on? Sometimes children want or need to say more, but also to have time to think through what they are going to say. If inadvertently their silence is misread as being time to move to the next part of the conversation, they will then be prohibited from exploring what they wanted to say and a further barrier will be erected.

Exercise

Practise incorporating silences into everyday conversations with family, friends and colleagues. As you do this, be aware of how it feels and what responses you get from the recipient. Does it feel uncomfortable and unnatural? Do you achieve more from the conversation by allowing silences to happen?

One of the main ways to facilitate the development of skills in communicating with this population of children is through the actual process of doing it. Undertaking a session and then reflecting on how it went are great tools for personal and professional learning. This is helpful even if you envisage that within your professional role you will be unlikely to come into contact with many children whose parents are dying. Reflecting on what went well, what could have been improved and what these improvements would look like are all strategies for helping to develop communication skills and good professional practice.

Practice point

Using colleagues as a resource can be beneficial in helping to develop confidence and competence in communicating with children. Their experiences of how they have developed and their ways of working can help inform practice. Also asking them for feedback about your practice could be a helpful and productive tool. Where appropriate, asking children for their feedback is also a good strategy for developing skills; children are generally very honest in their appraisal and if they think areas could be developed they will tell you! Asking them to rate you and to suggest ways that you could do things differently in subsequent encounters could be very enlightening. However, you need to be prepared to accept very honest observations – if you do not want to hear the answers, don't ask the questions!

Summary

Being included in conversations about the parent's illness is imperative in helping children begin to make sense of what is happening. Within this, they can begin to try to unravel the meaning behind all the different changes that they are witnessing within their family. However, barriers are often erected that prevent such conversations from being held. At times these barriers are created by the parents, for example:

- from a desire to protect their children

- because of a fear of upsetting them

- because of a belief that they are too young to know.

However, professionals also, at times, erect barriers for reasons of:

- protecting children

- protecting themselves

- not having time

- complex and complicated circumstances.

Whatever the roots of these barriers, it is important that the necessary skills are developed to help professionals develop their confidence and competence to become effective communicators.

This chapter has explored factors that are typically associated with parents' and professionals' construction of barriers and has also considered practical ways in which professionals can develop their communication skills. In the following chapter, one specific resource will be described along with detailed suggestions for its application when working with children whose parents are dying.

Chapter 4

The Communication Continuum

Background to the concept of the communication continuum

This chapter will introduce the communication continuum, which is a concept that offers a practical application to a model when thinking about the extent of children's involvement in the communication and information-sharing process. The idea of there being a communication continuum began to emerge from the rich accounts of the children and professionals involved in research (Fearnley 2010). The participants talked about how children are included or excluded from communication exchanges about their parent's illness and how this affects their understanding of what is occurring within their family (see Box 4.1 below). From these observations the idea that there is a communication continuum upon which children are 'placed' began to develop. The continuum can be used in a number of different ways. It can help practitioners to focus their thinking when assessing children's understanding of their current situation. Thinking about where the children are placed offers insight into how much information they have about the illness and its trajectory; this in turn can assist when planning work with them. The other primary application of the continuum is through practical use. It can be used as a tool when working with children to help them to say where they think they are positioned and also to begin thinking about where they would ideally like to be on the scale. This is important because all children will have different views about the amount of information they want or feel they require, and, although as professionals we may 'know' what is appropriate, children have the capability of knowing how much information they genuinely want and can emotionally cope with. Later in the chapter this will be discussed in more detail.

Children who were included in conversations about their parent's illness and who were regularly updated with information appeared to develop more robust strategies for making meaning from what was happening. Their narratives were richer and exemplified more mature coping mechanisms that had been developed as a result of their greater understanding of what was happening within their family. Conversely, children who did not enjoy such inclusions were the ones who had limited knowledge and awareness about what was occurring. These were the children who struggled to understand the situation, failed to develop an accurate appraisal and consequently had fewer opportunities to make meaning.

Children's positioning on the continuum

During the research, patterns began to emerge whereby children were placed at either the open or closed end of the continuum. Consequently, children are placed on the continuum in terms of their inclusion and awareness, and their positioning is determined by the quality and quantity of information they receive. Accordingly, the more they are involved, the more they enjoy an open awareness and are positioned towards the 'open' end of the continuum. Children who do not experience such levels of involvement are more likely to be placed at the 'closed' end of the continuum and have a closed awareness. This positioning has consequences in the short term during the illness but also following the death. In the research, bereaved children who had enjoyed a more open position tended to be able to articulate more positive coping strategies and enjoyed greater resilience in managing the situation. However, the bereaved children who had received little information, or inaccurate information, and who as a result were more towards the closed end of the continuum, tended to share stories of difficult grief and problems with coping during their bereavement. For the participants who were now young adults, this was a chronic situation that they struggled to manage, and which highlighted difficult and complex stories that were interspersed with uncertainty and unresolved grief.

The concept of this model has similarities with the work of Glaser and Strauss (1980) and their observations of communication styles between hospital personnel, patients and the patients' families. Their research suggests that within interactions between medical staff and patients there are four awareness contexts. These contexts range from a closed awareness, where the patient is not aware of their impending death despite the nursing staff being aware of it, through to an open awareness context where all involved know and acknowledge that the patient is dying. The communication continuum has similar core features insomuch as the extent of the communication the children enjoy plays a significant role in determining where they are placed on the continuum. Children who would be categorised as being in Glaser and Strauss's closed awareness would be towards the closed end of the continuum, whereas children enjoying an open context would be towards the open end of the continuum.

Features of the continuum

The children's positioning on the continuum is not static and they can move along it in both directions. This movement is determined by the amount of and quality of information the children receive. Therefore, if initially they are not included in conversations about the illness, they are likely to be placed at the closed end of the continuum. However, if their circumstances change and they become more involved, they have the potential to move along towards the open end. This possible movement emphasises the important role practitioners have in gently supporting parents to recognise the value of communicating with their children, along with the significance of professional intervention during the pre-death period.

Box 4.1: The communication continuum

The continuum is represented as a line where closed communication is at one extreme and open communication is at the other. In between these two extremes are differentiated points along the continuum:

- Totally closed communication – no information, no opportunities to share fears with anyone.

- Mostly closed – very little information, some opportunities to share fears.

- Partially closed – some information and some sharing, but highly coded and unclear; fears not recognised or dealt with.

- Partially open – some clear information but limited opportunities to share its meaning.

- Mostly open – regular updates of information and some opportunities to share knowledge with adults.

- Totally open – kept fully informed throughout and given open access to adults'/parents' feelings and responses.

This chapter will outline the concept of the communication continuum, children's movement along it, and how professionals can utilise the concept and support such movement by children.

Exercise

Sally's experience of living with a mother with cancer was introduced in Chapter 2. Where on the continuum would you place Sally? With the information you have about her experiences, would she be placed more towards the closed or open end of the continuum?

Comment: it is likely that Sally is placed towards the closed end of the continuum. She has only recently been included in conversations about her mother's illness and the information she has received has been vague and inconsistent. When she was initially told about her mother's prognosis, by the Macmillan nurse, she was given a large chunk of information by someone with whom she had not built up a relationship. The session had been subject to time constraints and there had been no time allocated to allow her to ask questions or explore her feelings. It would appear that she had had limited opportunities to discuss the situation with either her parents or a professional and had not been given further information about what is happening.

Children's movement along the continuum – factors that help or hinder

Children's positioning on the continuum is determined by a number of interrelated factors and these will now be explored in more detail in this section. Although each section is presented separately, it should be acknowledged that these are not discrete and can work collectively to create a complex barrier that impedes children's movement along the continuum.

How information is given

How children are given information and by whom will inevitably have a bearing on their positioning on the continuum. If familiar adults, preferably their parents, include them and actively encourage them to be involved in what is happening, this will help in placing them at the open end. Likewise, if the professionals involved with the family feel confident in talking with the children in a matter-of-fact way, this again will help in the process. Conversely, when the children are included but by people they do not know or have a limited relationship with, this will affect their positioning.

How children hear the information will have an impact on their positioning. If the information is 'second hand' and comes from an unreliable source, there is the potential for them to be given misinformation and as a result to misinterpret it. Therefore, partial or inaccurate information can be as unhelpful as no information and the children will still be placed towards the closed end of the continuum. As Chapter 2 highlighted, 'stolen conversations' have the potential to provide limited and inaccurate information that will affect how children process and in turn manage the limited knowledge they have gleaned. This partial knowledge is likely to create misunderstandings and false perceptions. The children will use the small amounts of information that they have managed to glean and weave their own version of events from these observations. The accuracy of the information provided and the subsequent interpretations made are potentially erroneous. Again a consequence of this is that the children's positioning on the continuum will be towards the closed end and without appropriate support they will be given few opportunities to amend their conceptions and develop a more accurate narrative.

Vignette

Chandran, a boisterous eight-year-old, starts to become aware that something is wrong when his mother's outgoing personality changes. She has less energy and avoids engaging in the rough and tumble games that they previously enjoyed together. One morning, during the summer holiday, Chandran collects the post and leaves it on the kitchen table for his mother. He sees that there is a letter for her from the local hospital. Later that day, Chandran overhears a small segment of a telephone conversation between his mother and grandmother. His mother is visibly upset but, when she realises that Chandran has entered the room, she changes the subject and talks about the weather. Over the following weeks, Chandran notices that his mother has a number of hospital appointments and that she has not been into work. One day he overhears her talking to her manager; she tells him that she is unsure when or whether she will be returning to work. Chandran asks his mother what is wrong and she tells him that she is 'a bit run down'. Later that week, Chandran meets his schoolfriend and confides in him that he thinks his mother is really poorly and is going to die.

Observations of the vignette

Chandran would be placed towards the closed end of the continuum. He has been given no information from his family about what is happening to his mother but has accumulated a number of pieces of information that he has translated. He is aware that something is wrong and has immediately drawn a conclusion from the few facts he has assembled. In reality, Chandran's mother does not have a terminal illness; she is pregnant and is being monitored by the hospital because of experiencing a number of miscarriages. However, Chandran's story highlights how children will piece together the shreds of information that they have, and draw their own, misinformed, conclusions. Moreover, the vignette provides a timely reminder about the importance, for good professional practice, of not making assumptions without gathering facts and evidence first.

Adults' desire to protect children

The parents' and professionals' desire to protect the children will also have an impact on the information exchange and, as a consequence, where the children are placed on the continuum. It has been suggested previously that this protective behaviour, while being undertaken in the belief that it is in the best interest of the children, can actually be harmful and have negative consequences. The resultant lack of information forces them towards the closed end of the continuum and, for some children, they are at the far end where they are at risk of becoming invisible. They struggle to glean any snippets of information that may help them to develop a picture of what is happening. Invariably the fragments of information they do garner are nutritionally poor and offer few helpful components that can satisfy their needs. The desire of parents to protect their children is understandable; however, when professionals collude with this silence, questions of 'in whose best interest' need to be asked. Balancing the needs of the patient with family members is never easy and offers a potent mix of ethical dilemmas. Nevertheless, professionals should recognise that the children's interests need to be considered and given equal thought, and that within their role they have a moral responsibility to explore possible options. Randall and Downie (2005) provide an in-depth discussion about the ethical and moral dilemmas professionals face when giving information in palliative situations. However, their discussions do not extend to the debates and dilemmas relating to children within the family. Chapter 6 includes sections on who should be told and how that information should be given.

The professionals' role

The professionals' confidence and competence in communicating with children, along with the quality of their training, play a significant role in contributing to children's positioning on the continuum. This is closely related to a consistent theme in the book; after all, if professionals are confident in their practice and acknowledge that children have a right to information, they are more likely to challenge ideologies and in turn represent best interests. Practitioners from different professions may have contradictory opinions, and conflicts of interest may arise. For example, palliative care consultants are likely to have the best interest of their patients at the core, while a children's social worker's primary responsibility lies with the welfare of the children. These contrasting relationships are likely to result in a conflict of opinions. Professionals from both disciplines will present a valid argument based on the doctrine of their professional body; however, the 'heavyweight' medical argument is likely to beat into submission the 'softer' emotional and psychological debate.

The timing of information

The timing of the information sharing plays an important role in determining where children are placed on the continuum. When children are included from the early stages of the illness, they have more opportunities to accommodate the information and live with the knowledge that their parent is ill. However, this again opens up a major moral and ethical debate about whether children should be informed immediately about the illness. With the significant medical advancements that we are now witnessing, survival rates for many illnesses and diseases have improved dramatically. As a result, the chance of survival is increased and therefore the difficult question arises as to whether the children should know about their parent's illness. Moreover, the nature of some illness trajectories is such that often the patient makes a marked recovery following a period of being unwell. This then creates a sense of hope that their health will always improve and, when the recovery is not made, the children are not prepared for the death. The uncertainty with these trajectories also complicates the picture for clinicians about when to hold a conversation about the likelihood of death. However, as the previous chapters have described, the inevitable disruption and emotional conflict that the news of illness can bring to family life will be observed by the children who will begin to recognise that something is wrong. Therefore, while it is often felt that they should be protected from such news, it is probably less alarming for them to be given honest, accurate, incremental information. How this information sharing is managed is important and careful consideration needs to be given as to how much detail is provided so that too many facts are not presented too soon. During the early stages of the illness, being made aware that their mother or father is ill and receiving medical treatment is different from being told that they have a potentially terminal illness and that they are going to die. Here again is an example of small chunks of relevant information being given as appropriate. As new information comes to light about the illness and its prognosis, the children can be updated and kept informed. If the prognosis does not look positive, they can then be given this news and, although it will be distressing and something they would really not want to hear, it will not be such a devastating shock.

Professionals, especially medical and nursing staff, have a role here in exploring with the parents the value of preliminary discussions with their children. When parents receive the initial diagnosis and the enormity of the information needs to be assimilated, their natural reaction is often to protect their children. This protection is typically shown by shielding the children and trying to buffer them from the harsh realities of the situation. If, within the medical consultation, time was allocated to explore the emotional and social aspects of the news, the professionals would have a valuable opportunity to talk with the parents about the children in the family, their needs and how best the family could be supported from the outset. These preliminary, gentle discussions, encouraging the family to establish a communication plan with the children, would have positive consequences for the children both in the short and longer term. The significant benefits would be their placement, from the outset, towards the open end of the communication continuum and their involvement throughout.

The language used

Chapter 2 discussed the importance of age-appropriate language and how consideration needs to be given to the language used so that it is clear and not ambiguous or misleading. Talking to children in language that they do not understand generally means that they are unable to decipher what is being said and consequently misunderstand the information. Moreover, if children are unable to comprehend the conversation, they are likely to divert their attention to something else and not listen at all to what is being said. This then creates a barrier for them in relation to making some sense of what is happening and in turn exposes them to the risk of being placed towards the closed end of the continuum.

How language is used and the choice of words are important in helping children make meaning from what they are being told. This was illustrated in Chapter 2 where Sally overheard a discussion that contained euphemistic language and she became aware that a patient had 'gone to sleep'. If children are given information that is in some way coded in an attempt to buffer them from the realities of the situation, they will not have factual information and there will be a blurring of fact and fiction. This has the potential to displace them from the more open end of the continuum towards the closed end. A cursory observation here would be that the children have been given information; however, the quality of that information is open to question and consequently the true value of it is debatable. Although they are being given information, it is inaccurate, which is therefore counterproductive and consequently inadvertently places them towards the closed end of the communication continuum.

If information, in a variety of forms, is not readily available from key people, an important opportunity to develop ideas that contribute to the meaning-making process is lost. The analogy of a jigsaw is appropriate in developing this thinking. If each piece of the jigsaw represents a further piece of information that can help in the process of developing a wide range of discourses, the children will have a variety of opportunities to create a more durable understanding of what is occurring in the family. Consequently, by having information from different sources, including their parents, professionals and wider society, in the form of quality media representation of terminal illness and death, children are more likely to enjoy an open awareness context, be positioned towards the open end of the communication continuum and produce a more complete jigsaw.

Children making informed choices about their positioning on the continuum

Children's positioning on the continuum is by and large determined by the adults around them; however, they do, on occasions, have some control over how the communication exchanges are managed. Some children are likely to choose to stay towards the closed end. They are living in a paradoxical situation. They know that their parent is seriously ill but they would prefer not to face the issue. These children often have sufficient information to know what is happening but make an informed choice not to contemplate the situation consciously. If children make this decision and it is based on appropriate information, their choice needs to be respected. If they are made aware that support is available, as and when required, their preferred coping mechanism can generally be managed.

The overwhelming need to escape from the reality of parental terminal illness inevitably affects children at some point during this period. They may choose not to be included in conversations and appear to be deliberately avoiding what is happening. While it could be suggested that these avoidant behaviours are behaviours typically seen, particularly in young people, and represent a time in their development where they are moving from dependence to independence, evidence suggests that they are employing coping strategies to help them traverse the unfamiliar contours of their lives. Adopting strategies that allow them to move away from the situation permits them to revert back to their previously known life that represents order, safety and comfort. This notion is similar to the work of Stroebe and Schut (1999) and their dual process model of grief. Within this model, the authors assert that the bereaved oscillate between coping behaviours – loss orientation and restoration orientation. The former encompasses grief work while the latter includes making lifestyle adjustments and developing a new identity. Stroebe and Schut argue that it is important for the bereaved to take time off from the emotion of grief in order to cope with what has happened. In a similar way, children's avoidance of thinking about and being central to their parent's illness could be a protective psychological mechanism that allows them to move away temporarily from the uncertainty and pain to a safer, known environment, where they can re-charge their 'emotional batteries'. Furthermore, by having some 'non-illness' time, they can re-engage with their pre-illness identity and, albeit briefly, enjoy their preferred identity. Moreover, by adopting this oscillating behaviour they are exercising some control and autonomy over a situation where they tend to have very little control or autonomy.

Observers taking a different standpoint could propose that this behaviour is the children denying, to themselves, what is happening. However, as Silverman (2000) citing Weisman suggests, there are times when the dying and those around them live in 'middle knowledge', which is where they are aware of death but it stays in the background. She suggests that this middle knowledge 'means that we live with contradicting philosophies and with the flexibility to move among many ways and kinds of knowing' (p.13). Children's positioning on the communication continuum is dependent, in part, on the level of flexibility offered to them through the conversations they are included in and the quality of information they are offered. This contributes to their many ways and kinds of knowing, which in turn helps determine where they are positioned on the continuum.

In some circumstances, as well as protecting themselves, children will choose not to talk about the situation in an attempt to protect their family (Ribbens McCarthy 2007). Consequently, professionals need to be open to the idea that there are different reasons why children might appear to be avoiding the situation, and to be cautious before they place them towards the closed end of the continuum. They may actually be more towards the open end but have temporarily moved away from coping with the illness and reverted back to a pre-illness identity, or they could be deliberately protecting themselves and others from the reality of the situation. Therefore, here is a further example where professionals need to assess the situation carefully, not be judgemental in their practice and not draw hasty conclusions without ascertaining the facts first.

Children's positioning on the continuum

Where children are positioned on the continuum is associated with a number of factors, some of which have been explored earlier. This section will present examples of children's experiences and how these affect their positioning on the continuum.

Vignette 1

Miriam is a 14-year-old who lives with her mother and younger brother. Miriam's parents divorced two years ago and she sees her father regularly. Her parents have remained amicable for the sake of the children. Miriam's mother was diagnosed with renal disease three years ago. Her illness has progressively worsened and she is reliant on Miriam and her brother for a significant amount of care. Miriam is responsible for much of the housework and there are expectations that she provides some child care for her brother. Miriam is fully aware of her mother's illness and 'just lives with it'; however, nobody has ever explained the facts about the illness to her and she has no understanding of the serious nature of the condition or the chances of it considerably shortening her mother's life. Miriam's parents acknowledge that she is ill but have a mutual agreement not to talk about the illness and to protect the children as much as possible. Miriam's mother has been allocated a social worker from the adult disability team. He has never discussed the children's needs with Miriam's mother because he is *her* social worker, not the children's. The GP and specialist from the local hospital have not mentioned the children and in fact the specialist is unaware that Miriam's mother has children.

Vignette 2

John is a 12-year-old who attends his local comprehensive school. His father was diagnosed with motor neurone disease (MND) 18 months ago. John's family has always enjoyed a close relationship and his parents decided that he should be informed about his father's illness very soon after the diagnosis. John has had regular updates from them about his father's health, the treatment and prognosis, and he feels able to speak openly to both his parents. On a couple of occasions he has attended the local MND support group, where his parents are now active members. Staff at the hospital have been made aware, by his parents, that John is an integral part of the family and that he has been fully included. Moreover, John's mother has contacted the Motor Neurone Disease Association and received helpful written information for John to read.

Observations of the vignettes

Miriam and John represent the two extremes of the continuum. Although Miriam is aware that her mother is ill, she has no understanding of the serious nature of the illness or how it is life limiting. Her parents have made the decision to protect her and her brother from the worry associated with the illness and have excluded them from any opportunities to talk about the implications of living with renal disease. This conspiracy of silence has extended to the professionals involved with the family. Miriam and her brother are likely to be at the closed end of the communication continuum. They are aware that their mother is ill but the seriousness of the illness has not been discussed. The children have not been given any opportunities to talk about what is happening and have not received any information that could help them to begin to make some meaning from what is happening.

John's experience is very different from Miriam's. His parents made the decision to include him from the outset and have continued to offer regular updates about all aspects of the disease, its treatment and the likely outcomes. As a result of this inclusion, John feels able to ask questions and engage in discussions about his father's health and prognosis. John is placed at the open end of the continuum.

Both Miriam and John have the potential to move along the continuum, in either direction. With appropriate support from professionals involved in health and social care, Miriam could move towards the more open end of the continuum. Her parents have taken the decision that the children should be protected from the situation and should not be included in any information sharing about the illness. Members of the medical team involved with the family have not explored the family dynamics and therefore are unaware of the existence of Miriam and her brother. Their failure to assess the family's make-up has resulted in lost opportunities to recognise the needs of the children and to develop a communication plan. Furthermore, the social worker, who *is* aware of the children, has again not acknowledged them or explored with Miriam's mother what they know and how they are coping. The social worker and medical team are best placed to facilitate Miriam's movement along the continuum. They could initiate a conversation with Miriam's mother to explore what Miriam and her brother know about the situation. Through their tentative enquiries, they could explore the reasoning behind not telling the children and also gently suggest the benefits, for the children, of their being included. Once these conversations have been undertaken, and with the parents' consent, they could then explore opportunities to initiate conversations with the children and decide who this role should be assigned to. This would be a positive first step in including Miriam and her brother, to help them begin to make some meaning from their family's situation and to enable them to move along towards the open end of the communication continuum.

The following vignette demonstrates how children's movement along the continuum is not always necessarily towards the open end and that in fact its fluid nature means that they can also move from the open towards the closed end.

Vignette

John's parents continue to include him in discussions about his father's condition; however, John's behaviour changes and he becomes less responsive to these conversations. His questions become more sporadic and his parents observe that he is spending more time with friends away from the family home. They interpret this change in behaviour as John's indifference to the disease and begin to include him less frequently.

Observations of the vignette

John's change in behaviour could be the result of a number of different factors. He may be feeling that he has coped enough and wants to return to the pre-illness life where he felt secure. He could have decided that he has sufficient information and needs to invest time with his friends and peers. Alternatively, because of his stage of development, he might feel the need to become more private about his feelings and avoid any talk of illness. Whatever the causes of the changes are, how they are being interpreted by his parents could result in his being less involved. This then has the potential for him to slip down the continuum away from his established position and towards the closed end. If John's parents shared this change in behaviour with the staff at the hospital, the staff could begin to explore with them the antecedents to this change in behaviour, suggest possible reasons for it and look at ways of maintaining John's inclusion while recognising and respecting his wishes.

Practice point

When using the continuum, it is important to recognise that movement can be in both directions. Sometimes the movement towards the closed end is the result of conscious choice by the children, but at other times it is because of a reduction in the levels of information previously provided. It is therefore important when using the continuum as a tool not to make the assumption that movement will only be in one direction – towards the open end.

Miriam and John's experiences represent the two antitheses of the communication continuum; however, there are many points between the totally open or closed ends. Sally, whose story was first described in Chapter 2, is an example of where a child is placed towards the closed end of the continuum but is not completely at the end. She has been given limited information about her mother's illness and her family has started to recognise the need to include her in the situation. Although there is limited time now to work with Sally before her mother dies, there are some opportunities to help her explore her feelings and develop some more robust narratives about what is happening in her life. The observations of her behaviour suggest that she is frustrated by not being included and that this frustration is leading to anger. Because communication channels have been very limited, she has not had any opportunities to talk about what is happening, express her feelings or explore the magnitude of the situation. It is therefore important that work with her is undertaken as a matter of some urgency to help her explore her feelings in a safe environment and through this for her to begin to develop some meaning from her situation.

Vignette

After the incident where Sally's behaviour became aggressive at her mother's bedside, the social worker discussed the situation at the next multi-disciplinary team meeting. She expressed her concerns about Sally, particularly that she thought she was potentially at risk because of the current situation and her needs not being met. It was agreed that, with Sally's parent's consent, the social worker would spend some time with Sally. This support would include time for her in the Activity Room where a number of play and art and craft materials would be made available. The social worker was acutely aware that she had limited time to complete the work before Sally's mother died. She wanted to assess how much Sally genuinely knew about the situation, how she was managing and the extent of her resilience.

The social worker decided that she had developed a sufficiently good working relationship with Sally to allow her to begin the assessment immediately and without preliminary work. She used narrative play to allow Sally to begin to tell a story about her current situation (Cattanach 2007). Sally engaged quickly in the session and immediately chose the play figures and hospital set. She arranged the set so that a mummy figure was in the bed and a number of doctors and nurses were clustered a little way away. The doctors and nurses were deep in conversation, which Sally represented as mumbles in her play. Occasionally some of the words she spoke were very clear, including 'sick' and 'more tests'. Throughout this play scene, the mummy figure remained quietly in the bed. Some distance away was a small doll figure representing a child. The social worker observed how Sally carefully placed the child away from what was happening but within the room. The social worker was curious in her questioning and asked Sally what she thought the doll figure might be thinking while it was playing alone. Sally reflected that the figure often felt alone and that it was trying to understand all the things the doctors were saying. The social worker asked Sally what kind of things she thought the doll figure would like to hear. Sally sighed heavily when she responded by saying that the doll knew that the mummy was poorly but wanted to know more about what was happening and really wanted to ask questions. With this, Sally turned the doll figure away from the bed.

Observations of the vignette

During the session, the social worker used play as a medium to begin to assess Sally's understanding of the current situation and where she is placed on the communication continuum. The abstract tone of the conversation that the social worker adopted meant that she took a less personal perspective, thus moving the focus away from Sally to the doll figure. Sally was able to articulate, from the doll's perspective, her thoughts and feelings about the situation, and from this the social worker was able to begin her assessment of what Sally might be thinking about her current situation and where she might be placed on the continuum.

Situating their experience in different locales

It is important to recognise that children's positioning on the continuum can be determined by the different environments they inhabit. They may experience a closed position at home but a more open one, for example, at school. It could be that within the home environment there are limited opportunities to talk about the illness. The parents and other adult family members may have decided that the topic remains locked away and no one is given the opportunity to talk about what is probably uppermost in everyone's thoughts. However, a supportive teacher at school could have recognised that they are experiencing difficulties. Conversations with the teacher, to explore the issues and associated feelings, may provide the children with the only opportunity they have to express thoughts and emotions in a safe environment. As a consequence, when at school the children temporarily move more towards the open end of the continuum. Conversely, it could also be the situation where the children are enabled at home to have open discussions about the situation but that these conversations are stymied at school. Therefore, these children would oscillate between a more open position at home and a closed one at school.

Using the continuum in direct practice with children

When considering how the continuum could be used in practice, it is important to remember that it is a fluid resource and that children can move along it in both directions. If children are initially told about what is happening, they may be placed towards the open end, but, as John's circumstances illustrate, this can alter so that they move down the scale. Conversely, because children are initially towards the closed end of the continuum, this does not mean that they will not be able, with support, to move towards the open end.

When using the continuum as a practical application with children, a useful starting point is to ascertain where on the continuum they are positioned. This early assessment can be achieved by asking the parents relevant questions to find out what they think their children know about the situation and how much they have been told. Some parents will be cognisant of their children's knowledge and be able to offer a clear insight into how much the children know. However, research has shown that there is often incongruence between what the parents think the children know and what the children actually know (Welch, Wadsworth and Compas 1996). Therefore it is important also to meet with the children and talk to them about their understanding of their family's circumstances. Asking the children to tell you about their family, possibly alongside asking them to draw their family, will help in developing an understanding of where they are on the continuum. Introducing the idea of a genogram may be helpful and will provide the children with an opportunity to define their family as they see it, their position within the family and other potential supporters in the form of extended family members (refer to Chapter 5 for a detailed account of genograms). This could be helpful both before and after the death when additional familial support may be necessary. Chapter 5 will discuss in detail the resources available to practitioners for such exploratory work.

Careful planning and thought need to be given to how to approach this early assessment. Things that need to be considered include the age of the children, their developmental level and cultural background. In addition, consideration needs to be given to the family's composition. How many children are in the family and what are their ages? Will the work be completed with all the children together or will they be seen separately? Where does each of the children fit within the composition of the family? Is it the family's disposition typically to have a closed communication style? How much information have the children gleaned from 'stolen conversations' and consequently how accurate is that information? These different factors are likely to have an impact on where the children are positioned on the continuum, and they also have the potential to block any movement towards the more open end.

Planning the assessment

The planning of sessions that will assess where children are positioned on the continuum should be carefully thought through, especially in relation to how the resource will be utilised. The concept of the continuum can be used as a visual tool to help the children and worker engage with the idea of a fluid line where movement along it can be achieved. The basic principle of a line can be creatively developed so that it becomes, for example, a road where the metaphor of a journey can then be introduced, or is used to extend ideas from the children's play. Younger children in particular will find it helpful if they have something that is visual and real to help them conceptualise the idea of a line. However, older children are also likely to benefit from having a tangible 'something' as opposed to a mental image.

Asking children where they think they are currently placed on this journey is a helpful starting point when assessing their position on the continuum. It is important here to be vigilant and to listen attentively to their discourse. Is their body language congruent with what they are telling you? How are they saying what they are saying?

Exercise

If you were working with Miriam, how do you think she might describe her positioning on the continuum? How might Miriam's discourse and behaviour differ from John's?

Comment: it would be expected that John would show more confidence when talking about where he thought he was placed on the continuum. His body language would reflect this and he would have the vocabulary to describe what was happening in his family. It is likely that he would be more positive in his discussions and also probably more assertive in deciding where he was placed. On the other hand, Miriam would be likely to show less confidence when talking about her positioning. This is because she has had fewer opportunities to talk about what is happening with her mother and family. These limited opportunities could mean that she has not been able to begin to make any meaning from what is happening and as a result has an impoverished script to work from. However, both children's responses are likely to be influenced by the relationship that they have, or have not, developed with the worker. If the children do not feel that they trust the worker, their responses are likely to be more guarded.

Once the worker has assessed where the children would place themselves on the continuum, the attention can then move to where they would like to be and how this might be achieved. Asking questions about where they would like to be on this journey will then offer some indications about how much information the children actually desire about their parent and the illness and, importantly, where they would choose to be positioned if they had a choice.

Introducing the idea of having a 'magic wand' can be a very useful tool in the worker's repertoire. The magic wand has similar properties to the well-established 'miracle question' that is regularly employed in narrative therapy (Freeman *et al.* 1997). Similarly, the magic wand has the 'power' to transport children, on the communication continuum, to a position where they would rather be. Direct questioning about this preferred place might not produce any answers; after all, children who have not been included previously will not necessarily have contemplated that there could be alternative positions available. Therefore, the magic wand helps them in a safe way to express their wishes while offering an insight to the worker about where they are on the continuum and where they would like to be. However, it is noteworthy that even with such magical powers some children are likely to place themselves away from the open end of the continuum. Knowing everything is sometimes just too difficult to contemplate.

Children's descriptions of where they would ideally like to be on the continuum provide a starting point for working together to try to reach that position. However, for this to be achieved, the parents need to give consent to any work being undertaken and also recognise that they have a significant role in supporting and helping their children. It is therefore important that the need for communication is discussed with the parents and that they have the opportunity to explore the benefits of including their children. Introducing the communication continuum to the parents, and within this providing examples of scenarios that affect children's positioning on the continuum and the longer-term consequences, would therefore be beneficial.

After parental permission for the work to be undertaken has been given, the worker can begin to develop strategies for working with the children. Different aspects of the situation may have been highlighted when using the continuum. For example, a priority could be to provide the time and a safe environment for the children to talk about what is happening. If they have been living in a communication vacuum, which invariably would place them towards the closed end of the continuum, having the opportunity to talk about all that is occurring, and to begin, through this, to make some meaning, is helpful in the move along the continuum.

The children may have identified that the lack of opportunities to explore the social and emotional changes that are occurring in their family is the major barrier to their moving along the continuum. In these circumstances, the focus of the work can be directed towards exploring emotions with the intention of unblocking feelings that will consequently allow them to move towards a more open position on the continuum.

Being given the opportunity to contemplate the future and what that future might look like could assist children to move towards the open end of the continuum. Beginning to think about one week, one month or one year ahead will help them to attach meaning to what is happening. For many children a concern, when living with a parent who is dying, is about the future. Questions about who will care for them, where they will live and how their lives will change are not uncommon. Children like predictability, routines and boundaries; however, the massive changes that families face when a parent is terminally ill have the potential to rock all that is known and safe (Saldinger *et al.* 2004b). Therefore, if the children can begin to think about what the future will hold for them and their family, they can begin to develop a narrative that has some substance and meaning.

It is equally possible that some children will not be able to identify anything specific that will help them move along the continuum. In these circumstances, giving them time to explore their feelings and to talk, with someone who genuinely wants to listen, may be all that is required.

Exercise

Reflect on a piece of work you have been involved with where a parent was terminally ill. How could you have implemented the communication continuum? Would there have been any potential obstacles? What additional resources would you have required?

Being able to reflect on past experience, and through this incorporate potentially new tools for working, can be helpful in developing skills, confidence and competence. The communication continuum is a tool that can be used for assessment but also creatively with children to help them develop some meaning from the situation and thereby establish stronger, more accurate narratives.

Summary

This chapter has introduced a practical resource that can be used both in the assessment of children's understanding and awareness of their current situation and as a therapeutic tool. Where children are placed on the communication continuum is largely determined by the amount of information about their parent's illness and prognosis to which they are privy. Children who are positioned towards the open end are the ones who generally receive more age-appropriate information and who are included in conversations about the illness. Conversely, children at the opposite end tend to be excluded from information and are not encouraged to talk about what is happening. Research would suggest that children who are towards the open end are more likely to find positive coping strategies and to be more resilient. Moreover, where children are on the continuum during the illness will be a factor in determining how well they manage, or do not manage, the situation following the death.

The chapter has outlined a number of factors that help or hinder the children's positioning on the continuum. These include:

- the quality and quantity of the information

- where the information comes from − is it a reliable source or is it second-hand information that could be misleading and inaccurate?

- the adult's desire to protect children from the reality of what is occurring

- the professionals' competence and confidence in communicating with children

- how the information is given, including the timing and delivery (in small or large chunks)

- the use of ambiguous and euphemistic language.

The positioning on the continuum is largely determined by the adults involved with the children. However, on occasions, children will make a conscious decision to be towards the closed end. They may choose to distance themselves from this incomprehensible situation and to move back into a pre-illness identity. Sometimes this is so they can re-charge their emotional batteries and sometimes it is about asserting some control over a situation where they have very limited control. Whatever the reasoning, if they are sufficiently informed about what is happening and are aware that support is available if required, this deliberate shift should be respected.

Chapter 5

Talking to Children

Stephanie Barker and
Rachel Fearnley

It has been asserted throughout this book that serious or life-threatening illness has an impact on all family members. Given this position, this chapter focuses on how parents can support and nurture family life in the face of adversity. The approach taken is how professionals can use communication to build on family strengths and resilience rather than adopting a problem-solving model. This may be a new way of working for many families who have been used to being seen and cared for within a medical model of healthcare where identifying the problem is the norm. This chapter is not meant as a comprehensive therapeutic cookbook but more as a range of condiments that can add depth and flavour to the existing dish. The resources outlined are ones that a variety of practitioners working in health, social care and education can incorporate into their practice to a greater or lesser extent.

Within the chapter we will again use vignettes to illustrate examples from practice. These will incorporate ways of working across a range of ages and all can be adapted to a variety of work settings.

Listen to me

The importance of communicating with children has been discussed throughout the book and, as we have seen, is pivotal in helping them begin to make some meaning from the situation of living with a parent who is dying. It is equally important that people listen to children and truly hear what they are saying. Having the opportunity to talk to someone who genuinely cares and is interested is so important for children navigating the alien landscape of parental terminal illness. The silencing of children's voices generally causes them to feel less important, unworthy and insignificant. A continued silencing renders them powerless and unable to communicate their feelings or needs, often to the extent where they are unable to recognise what these feelings are. Brookes (2006), writing specifically about children in research, offers a succinct reminder that when children are included in research they do not 'just demand free Smarties but respond with astonishing maturity according to the circumstances in which they find themselves' (p.13). Similarly, when children are enabled to have a voice, they are capable of articulating clearly their wishes, hopes and worries. However, for this to be achieved, there need to be people around them who will make time to listen, to encourage them to express their thoughts and to facilitate this uni-directional exchange.

Having a voice

Having a voice and being able to verbally express feelings, thoughts and emotions enables children to develop more robust narratives about their experiences. They are able, through the two-way process, to explore what is occurring and from this incorporate the ideas into their biography. Having a voice is therefore a significant piece in the children's jigsaw and without it they will not be in a position to produce a complete picture. Moreover, having a voice and being heard is important in relation to addressing the power imbalance that children, who are marginalised because of parental terminal illness, often experience. There is often a tendency, at the levels of both policy and practice, for children within the family to be unnoticed and consequently their views ignored. This was highlighted by Chowns (2008) who argues that 'children are largely seen but not heard in palliative care' (p.16). Goodwin and Horowitz (2002) question whether there are 'groups whose voices we do not (or cannot) hear' (p.39). It would appear that this observation is most salient when thinking about the experiences of children living with a dying parent. Moreover, when consideration is given to children's experiences, it is generally explored through the views and understandings of their adult caretakers (Christensen and James 2001). The adult's voice takes precedence and the children are silenced by societal beliefs, values and often, sadly, ignorance.

Blocking children's voices and preventing them from having opportunities to express their ideas can be likened to damming a stream. While the flow of water may be initially held back, it will eventually find another course and seep out. Children, at different developmental stages, will have different approaches within their arsenal to make it known that they want to be heard and to find ways of 'seepage'. The frustrations of not being heard and not having a voice are too frequently observed as their being 'angry young people' attempting to get their views across. However, this anger may be misunderstood by observers: it is generally a result of frustration and a strong desire to have the opportunity to make their voices heard. When such opportunities are thwarted, the need remains and other outlets are sought.

When opportunities for verbal expression are stymied, children will often resort to displaying their feelings through behaviour, which generally is seen as being 'inappropriate'. Children in my research described how their anger at the situation, and the lack of opportunities to be heard, resulted in their becoming aggressive and participating in risk-taking behaviours. One young person candidly observed how they had become 'quite horrible to everybody' and another talked about being unkind to others while expecting them to be kind to them.

Speaking on behalf of the children

Adults involved with children have a responsibility to facilitate the children's voices but they can also significantly contribute to the silencing of them. Parents will often talk for the children and become their voice. Within this, parents represent the views, thoughts and feelings of their children and thus silence them. This is something of which professionals, working with the family, need to be cognisant. Within conversations, are the children given opportunities to describe how they are feeling or to explore their emotions? Have parents developed well-practised tactics for representing their children's views and has this style become the dominant feature of all communication exchanges? Are there opportunities available for the children to have a voice or are they silenced by their physical absence? If professionals only meet with patients and their partners during school hours, there are fewer opportunities to see the children and hear their voice. These are important issues, which should be reflected upon when working with families, and, if the assessment is that the adults are rendering the children silent, then the professionals should consider ways they can help to make the children's voices heard.

Sometimes in family cultures the discourse is hierarchical and, as a consequence, older or more dominant children will speak on behalf of their siblings, or the males will speak on behalf of the females within the family. This can have the powerful effect of rendering siblings silent and their views either misrepresented or not represented at all. Being aware of this when working with families is helpful and again will help professionals to assess who has a voice and who interprets for others within the family construct.

What the voice sounds like

When thinking about children having a voice, it is always important to consider what they may want that voice to sound like. It would be ineffective practice to make the assumption that there is a correlation between giving children opportunities to have a voice and their fluently expressing themselves. Sometimes children will want and need to talk about things that appear unrelated to the current situation. A pressing concern for a six-year-old may be the uncertainty of being invited and able to attend a friend's birthday party the following week. While this may appear to be a trivial matter, to the child it could be of utmost importance. For other children, being able to revert back to a pre-illness identity means that their discourse may also be unrelated to their parent's illness. Having the opportunity to talk about issues other than the illness is important in grounding the children in their current preferred identity. If children are aware that opportunities are available for them to discuss the illness and its implications, along with talking about life outside illness, they will know that they can select appropriate moments to explore feelings and thoughts about what is happening in their lives. A key factor here is having a 'fellow traveller' alongside them who is receptive and will encourage these conversations when the children are ready to have them.

It is important, therefore, that professionals working with children have an understanding of the different ways they cognitively process what is happening, as well as how they cope and manage their situations.

Some children may want to use their voice to explore cause and effect: 'Did Mummy have a heart attack because I was naughty?', 'Will I catch what Daddy has got?' And some may want to use these opportunities to make some sense of what is happening. Being able to encourage their voice, in whatever form it appears, is an important function of professionals working alongside children. Being attuned to the voice of the child is a skill that can be developed and one that is really vital to an effective communicator. It is generally acknowledged in post-modern Britain that children have a right to be heard and to discuss freely matters that are relevant to their life experiences. This is never truer than when they are living with a parent who is dying and their worlds have been turned upside down.

Helping children find a voice

When a parent is first diagnosed with a serious or life-threatening illness, the first task is to assimilate and make sense of this news and its implications. A myriad of questions is likely to be formulated ranging from 'What next?', 'What does this diagnosis mean?', 'What treatment will I have to have?' to 'Will I get better?' All these questions are part of the information context of what people want and need to know. More difficult to answer are the equally important questions that have a more emotional focus, such as 'What am I going to tell my children?', 'Will I die?' and 'What is going to happen to my children?' What we know is that healthcare professionals are more likely to address questions about diagnosis and treatment than they are about emotional and psychological consequences of hearing devastating news. This may be in part due to either an unwillingness to 'open up Pandora's box', a perceived time issue or a lack of either skill or confidence in addressing these important matters (Mitchell 2010). So this means that, while professionals may respond to the questions raised by patients that focus on feeling rather than fact, they are unlikely to be proactive in raising the issue for themselves. This is important work to do, for it is unreasonable to expect any individual to attend to the difficult task of talking to children about serious illness and possibly dying until they have reached a sufficient level of knowledge and understanding about what diagnosis and treatment might mean. Similarly, there are other stages at which a reappraisal and re-evaluation of treatment and disease progression may be required. Particularly challenging times can be when a patient makes the transition from living with illness to recurrence of disease, worsening of their condition or, most significantly, the recognition that they are in the palliative or final stages of their illness and approaching death.

One of the biggest challenges to emotional well-being can be living with uncertainty and this holds true for children as well as adults, so one can understand that many parents will try and put off having this very difficult conversation thinking that, in some way, not talking protects their children from emotional distress. But do children know that all is not well? It can be difficult to hide the physical consequences of treatment. For example, any patients undergoing a course of chemotherapy may experience either hair loss or a range of symptoms such as tiredness, nausea or low spirits. What we often find is that children have a sense of 'knowing' even if they do not 'know' the right things. If left unaddressed, misunderstanding or misinterpretation can give rise to high levels of distress or worry. The distress can manifest itself in a number of ways ranging from emotional withdrawal and regressive behaviours to obvious symptoms of anxiety and depression (Christ 2000a). The challenge here is to help children understand what is happening in a way that is appropriate for their age and cognitive development.

So how do we help children to 'know'?

Establishing a therapeutic relationship

As in any relationship, the first step is to establish a rapport with the child. This can be difficult when the practitioner is working in a setting that tends to exclude children. To what extent do we make adult hospital wards or clinics user-friendly from a child's perspective? This is less an environment question than one of systems. Flexible hospital visiting hours would take account of the school day or the needs of young children to have structured early evening routines of care. However, the reality is that many hospitals operate a visiting policy that primarily (and not unreasonably) meets the needs of adults and clinicians. This does have the potential of leaving children separated from a parent sometimes for a protracted period of time.

Exercise

Look at your place of work through the eyes of a child. How friendly and welcoming is it? What would you want to change? What would be the resource implications?

Children can be naturally curious about what happens to their mummy or daddy when they go to hospital for an investigation or treatment, and the question might be raised about whether parents are actively encouraged to let children come and look around the place where treatment takes place. The opportunity to look and see where mummy goes every three weeks to have chemotherapy can be invaluable in helping to dispel myths or alarming fantasies. It also gives children the opportunity to meet with nurses and doctors who are taking care of their parent, and sets the scene for conversations about illness and treatment.

Many practitioners find it easy to respond to the question that family members (including children) ask, particularly if the response requires factual information. What is more difficult is *creating* opportunities for serious conversations to take place, especially if the practitioner has medical information that leads them to believe that things are getting worse for the patient. In these circumstances, there is a higher probability that some of the questions being formulated by the patient are ones that are much more difficult to answer.

Exercise

Take an example of a patient having a second course of chemotherapy. A child asks two questions, 'How does chemotherapy work?' and 'Will the chemo make my mummy better?' Which one is easier to answer and why?

Comment: to answer the second question may involve preparing a child for the possibility that the chemotherapy may not work and mummy might die. It is more likely that the child will ask the more emotionally laden second question when they have built up a rapport with the practitioner and have been given clear signals that it is okay to ask such a question. It is important to remember that the non-verbal cues we give off either encourage or discourage emotional disclosure. Looking at your watch or making little or no eye contact can be very clear signals of unwillingness to engage in conversation and even very small children can recognise this lack of interest. The net result can be to close down the opportunity for significant and helpful conversations to take place. This can be related to the discussion in Chapter 3 about the barriers that are sometimes erected by adults when talking to children, and which give strong messages about not wanting to develop the conversation.

Being 'in tune' with children

If the practitioner keeps up to date with popular television programmes including soap operas and reality shows, it can be a great way to open up a conversation. Part of this early intervention is respecting when children want to talk and when they do not. Taking time to build up a therapeutic relationship can pay dividends. Questions to children formulated through natural curiosity about their interests can result in the building of trust, understanding and a spirit of collaboration. Family therapists often refer to this phase as 'joining' and this seems a good word to sum up the way in which a practitioner gets to know and to make a connection with each member of a family. Sometimes there can be a whole series of brief exchanges before children can 'warm up' enough to have anything that remotely resembles a fully formed conversation!

Working in community settings

Those practitioners working in community settings are better placed to meet with children in a context where they might feel safest and most secure – that is, the home. This time the question might be do you visit your patient during the day or do you wait until the end of the afternoon when the children might be home from school? Being able to meet with children in surroundings that are familiar to them and talk to them about day-to-day subjects such as their favourite football team or television programme, their interests and hobbies, and how they are getting on at school can be a great way of beginning the engagement process that is so important for good communication to occur.

Exploring patterns of communication within a family

When working with all family members, it becomes easier to establish the way in which they communicate together. Is this a family where everyone listens respectfully to each other or does everyone need to shout to get their voice heard? Is this a family that uses emotionally expressive language or do family members find it difficult to express their thoughts and feelings? Is this a family where there are high levels of cohesion or is conflict and rowing the norm? Is this a family that works well together to problem solve or does adversity result in domestic chaos? Do some family members collude with others? By observing these different dimensions of family communication, it enables practitioners to adjust their own patterns of intervention so that they become more useful in helping the family to talk together. Every family is different and so the notion that one size fits all cannot be applied.

Vignette

Susan, aged 43, is married to David and has two boys, aged 11 and 13. She was diagnosed with autoimmune liver disease ten years ago and has recently been told that this has progressed to cirrhosis for which a transplant is the only possible treatment. Susan asks Jenny, a specialist nurse, to help her with the task of telling the boys the news. Together they agree what information to give them and Susan rehearses how she will do this. Jenny's role is to be available to answer any questions that the children may have relating to treatment in the future. Jenny has seen both boys on a number of occasions before and has observed that they constantly argue with one another and that the only way in which Susan can get them to be quiet is to shout at them.

Exercise

What might Jenny need to consider and do to facilitate this family to begin talking together about serious illness?

Observations of the vignette

Jenny might need to take some time to explore and establish the ground rules for talking together. This could include a collaborative conversation about how everybody's voice can be heard. One tool Jenny could possibly select is an object that can be used as a 'talking stick', whereby the person who is holding the talking stick is the only one who is allowed to talk. When the person has finished, the stick is passed to the next person who can then talk. Anything at all can be used to represent the talking stick and often the more ridiculous choice, the better, because it taps into the playful world of children. An alternative can be to take a little time for the children to make their own talking stick. If children are left to their own devices to design and make the stick, you need to be prepared for an extravaganza of glitter glue, feathers and dried pasta!

While in the vignette it is a specialist nurse who has been co-opted to help, in our experience it is equally likely that Susan might ask any professional to help with this work, particularly if she has a good relationship with them.

Talk about talking

Another element of rule setting is to 'talk about talking'. This might mean establishing an overview of some of the things everyone feels comfortable with and wants to talk about, but also getting a clear idea of those topics that some members of the family may not be ready to discuss. It can be difficult to predict how conversations will develop and so another safeguard with children is to establish some kind of signal that allows them to indicate that they want to stop talking or change the direction of the conversation. In a room where there are two adults and two children, the balance of power is likely to be with the adults and their agenda rather than with the children. It is important to recognise ways in which the balance of power can be made more equal and the stop signal is one way of achieving this. The practitioner also has the responsibility to be sensitive to the non-verbal cues children give that they want to stop talking. This may be through disengagement, disruptive behaviours or very obvious cues such as covering their ears with their hands.

Whose responsibility is it?

From the point of diagnosis onwards, adults with serious and long-term illness will come into contact with a large number of professionals who may play a part in supporting both the individual and the family members. In some cases this will be a long relationship. School provides an enduring source of support for children so it is important to encourage parents to update the school about the progress of their illness if they have not already done so. The teacher is in an ideal position to respond by asking, 'What exactly have you told your child and how have they reacted?' This enables the teacher to offer ongoing support in ways that are consistent with the child's current understanding. It also helps identify the individual emotional support children may require. It is important that the teacher is made aware of areas of sensitivity for the child so that distress is not inadvertently triggered. An example of this would be where a classroom activity is to write about a favourite family holiday at a time when the child's parent is deteriorating and losing independence. This may make a connection for the child to all the family activities that are currently being lost as a consequence of the changing nature of illness.

The approach of checking and rechecking what the children know and understand on a regular basis, particularly at transitional points when the symptoms of illness increase, is one that can and should be adopted by any professional working regularly with a family. It is also a question that should be uppermost in the mind of anyone who comes into contact, in a professional capacity, with an identified patient at any point in the illness pathway.

Some general rules for talking with children

If conversations about serious illness are best held with people you trust, then for most children this would be the parent. However, in the same way that parents want to protect their children from sadness and distress, often children also want to do the same for the ill and well parent. This is particularly the case with young people who have the maturity to understand the impact that their emotional well-being (or otherwise) may have on their parent. Under these circumstances it could be helpful for children to talk with a professional who can address their questions in an honest and sensitive manner but, more importantly, can hold their distress. Many parents may have told their children about the illness and treatment. Some may have discussed the implications for the future, particularly if their children are teenagers. What is often requested from the practitioner is that they engage with the children to explore their current understanding of the information they have been given. This is an opportunity to correct any misunderstanding that they might have.

Practice point

As professionals, we can often get embroiled in the practice of doing things for others so that we lose sight of the fundamental truth that in some circumstances we do not have to 'do' anything. More important is the capacity just to listen, hear and acknowledge what has been said.

Preparing to work with the children

In getting started, the essential skill of developing rapport with children has already been highlighted. If an important conversation about health and illness is going to take place, practitioners should make clear from the outset what their role is and the type of questions that they may be able to answer, because this helps to set a framework for the session. Clarifying the timeframe can also be very useful for children: 'I'd like to talk to you about your mum; is that okay? I thought we might chat for about ten minutes but I have got more time either today or next week if we need it.' In this short sentence a tone of informality has been set, the children have had their permission sought for the conversation to take place, they know that they do not have to talk for a long time but also that they are not going to be closed down if they have a lot that they want to say.

If the children are reluctant to have a conversation at all, it is important not to take this at face value but to explore why this might be. It may be they want to do something else that they see as being more important – for example, watching a favourite television programme – so the timing is not right. Or it may be that emotionally or psychologically they do not feel ready to talk and this should be respected. To be truly collaborative, it may be useful to ask if there is a time or place where it might be easier to talk. Remember that having conversations in small chunks, especially for younger children, will help them to absorb and process the information more easily.

As professionals we often have our own agenda of what we want to achieve during any consultation but when we work with children it is important to recognise that we may only achieve a fraction of what we want to in any one session. A key skill for practitioners is to know when to stop. If a child is showing any signs of disengagement, then respectful and ethical practice should tell us to bring the conversation to an end for the day. If building a rapport has been very successful, small children may want to engage you in all kinds of playful activities rather than talk. Under these circumstances, it may be possible to negotiate two to five minutes of more focused conversation in return for ten minutes of play! Pacing is key either in the one-off session or over longer-term work because it respects the children's position and gives them some power within the therapeutic relationship.

Confidentiality

It has already been highlighted that there is a tendency for children to protect their parents from the additional distress that disclosing their own worries and concerns might create. Under these circumstances, the aim of therapeutic intervention on the part of the practitioner is to promote disclosure, and to hear the children's voice while recognising the need to keep some things private from their parents. At the beginning of the conversation it is important to be clear about the bounds of confidentiality for both the children and the parents. The general rule is that anything said by the children will not be shared with the parents unless permission has been given to do so. However, it is important to make explicit that there are circumstances when this rule has to be broken. A reason may be that during the conversation it becomes clear that the children's emotional response to what is happening within the family in relation to health and illness is resulting in risk-taking behaviours, which might include self-harm or suicidal ideation. Wherever possible, the aim should be to encourage shared disclosure with the parents but, if the children are unable to do this, the practitioner has a responsibility to do so. In this case, practitioners should tell the children what they are about to do and why, explaining that it is in their best interests. However, it could also be that, from the conversations, a practitioner becomes aware that there are concerns that the child is at risk of harm as defined by the Children Act 1989. In such cases, appropriate action, following the local Safeguarding Children Board's procedures, has to be followed.

Before any conversation takes place between practitioners and children, it can be very helpful if parental support for a private conversation is clearly given by the parent. Parents are powerful role models and their own response to talking about difficult issues can make it easier or harder to talk with children. Being given permission to talk by a parent can be one of the most powerful ways of helping children to find their voice and, similarly, not being encouraged to talk can have the effect of silencing them.

Roles and responsibility

It is important to remember what the professional's roles and responsibilities may be in relation to talking with children about serious illness. At the very least, it may be to proactively raise the question with parents, 'What have you told/what do your children understand about your illness?' Alternatively, it may entail direct conversations with children about what is happening to mum or dad. It can be argued that the former approach should come within the remit of any healthcare practitioner because it recognises the importance of the family as the unit of care. Working directly with children may possibly be seen as a more specialist role and it is important that all practitioners working at this level recognise the limits of their own competence and know how and whom to refer on to if the child or family need more specialised psychotherapeutic intervention. When beginning any work with children, it is imperative that workers are honest about their involvement and that they do not make any promises to children that are unrealistic and cannot be honoured. For example, when in dialogue with children, telling them that their parent's health will improve and that they will get better, when it is evident that they are going to die, is very poor practice.

Resources
Child-focused practice

In her study of 88 families (157 children) who coped with the impact of terminal illness and the death of a parent, Christ (2000a) plotted the stage of the parent's illness against changes in the children's development. By breaking the data down into age groups, there is more clarity from the results. Strikingly, Christ found that the children's anticipatory grief was more stressful than the actual death and she argues that before death is the time for intervention. The reality and paradox of clinical practice is that, in a bid to protect children from the pain and sadness of impending death, not addressing the issue ultimately results in crisis work with them and high levels of emotional distress. In Stephanie Barker's inpatient unit it is not uncommon to find that adults are admitted for end of life care but no explicit conversation about illness or dying has taken place with their children or grandchildren. An extreme example of this was where a young man was admitted and deteriorated rapidly. In the space of eight hours we had to support his son aged six as he made the painful transition from not knowing anything was seriously wrong to having to say goodbye to his father. Moore, Pengelly and Rauch (2010) reflect on the potential for communication to affect the psychological adjustment of children.

The conversations with children and their families are likely to fit into one of three categories:

1. getting information

2. giving information

3. exploring thoughts, concerns and feelings.

Every family and every child in a family is different and so this is not a cookbook approach to working with children; rather, it is a selection of ingredients that can be put together in creative and imaginative ways, which result in helpful and meaningful dialogue. Being flexible and responsive is central to effective practice in this field.

Getting information
Genograms
A genogram is one of the most useful tools in palliative care. They are often used within medicine as a quick and easy way of plotting health and illness within a family. It is an extended version of using a family tree but has the added advantage of helping the practitioner to explore the nature of relationships within any given family. This can be particularly useful when you consider the impact that serious illness can have on family functioning. Detailed accounts of how to construct a genogram can be found in several family therapy textbooks – for example, McGoldrick, Gerson and Petry (2008).

The initial part of constructing a genogram is fairly straightforward and consists of elucidating information about who is in the family, demographic characteristics such as marriages, civil partnerships, separation, divorce, occupation and geographical location. Other life events such as illness, death, redundancy or periods of unemployment can also be elicited. When focusing on current illness a number of questions can be framed:

- When did the illness first start?

- How was the illness first noticed or diagnosed? What were the symptoms? Have these symptoms changed over time?

- What (if anything) does the illness get in the way of? For instance, does it stop you or any family member from doing anything?

- Has anything changed in your family since illness came into your lives?

- How did your family react when you were told about the illness? (If the answer to the question is, for example, anger, you might want to explore how anger shows itself in every family member. This could be followed up by a scaling question, 'Who was the most angry, least angry?') How would you have wanted them to react? (This type of approach works well for a wide variety of emotional responses.)

- Have roles and responsibilities in the family changed since the illness was diagnosed?

- Who talks most about the illness? Who does not talk about the illness?

These are only a few of the questions that can be asked to add detail to the genogram and give the practitioner a much deeper understanding of the impact the illness has had on all family members. Externalising language is used to describe 'the' illness rather than personalised language such as 'your' illness. This makes it much easier for families to talk together in a way that does not attribute any blame or responsibility. Many adults feel very guilty that their illness has had a profound impact on all the family. Completing a detailed genogram takes time and requires considerable skill from the practitioner. However, the above questions offer a framework that will be sufficient for most assessments by health and social care professionals.

Wherever possible it is useful to have several family members involved in creating the genogram because this adds to the richness of detail and offers the opportunity to hear several perspectives of the same story. When constructing this map of family life, it is important to be tuned to what is not being said as well as what is. Careful observation of non-verbal cues can give the practitioner an idea of those areas of family life or the illness experience that are less easy to talk about. It may be appropriate to acknowledge overtly that this seems difficult or, alternatively, tactfully to change the focus of questioning. There are times when information is gathered that the family does not want recorded on a genogram, particularly if it is of a sensitive nature. For example, when obtaining information about when children were born, an adult may mention a child from a previous relationship who has been adopted. While the partner may know this, it may not necessarily be common knowledge to other family members. Given that this is a family document, the adult may request not to have the information added to the family genogram and this should be respected.

Vignette

Lucy, whom we met in Chapter 3, is observing her manager, Annabel, who is making an assessment using a genogram. Using the type of questions outlined earlier, Annabel establishes that Michelle is a 39-year-old woman married to David and together they have three children: a daughter Lily aged 14, and two sons John and Harry aged 11 and 7 respectively. Michelle had been diagnosed with heart failure three years previously and over this period she has become increasingly symptomatic, getting very short of breath with the slightest exertion. She and David married 15 years ago and at that point Michelle gave up work as a secretary to set up home for her husband. Both she and David were devastated at the initial diagnosis and her symptoms of anxiety and distress have become worse over the three-year period. They both identify that currently their main source of difficulty is their daughter Lily because she is refusing to do many of the household tasks they allocate to her. If she does do them, it is only after shouting and screaming at both her parents. This is causing high levels of tension in the family and has resulted in Michelle and David frequently referring to her as 'that idle monkey'. Lucy observes that Lily remains sullen and withdrawn throughout the process of constructing the family genogram. Both parents appeal to Annabel to 'talk some sense into this selfish girl!'

Exercise

What thoughts do you have about the roles and responsibilities within the family, and what might be helpful interventions here?

Outcome of Annabel's assessment

Michelle has always identified herself as a mother, a role with its attendant responsibilities that she has always taken seriously. It is very difficult for her to see her house untidy. David hates to see his wife so distressed by this and his problem-solving nature believes that all will be well if Lily just takes on the tasks that her mother cannot do. Not only does this involve housework but also a responsibility for caring for her younger brothers, which includes enforcing rules about family behaviour such as getting them to wash their hands before they have their meals. For her part, Lily does not want this additional responsibility – she just wants to go and hang out with her friends as many 14-year-olds do. What seems to be happening here is that, because of illness, Lily is expected almost to co-parent her younger siblings with her father because her mum is unable to do this.

What would be helpful here would be to deconstruct the idea of being 'an idle monkey'. What does it mean? The family's belief system is that men should go to work and earn money to keep the family financially secure and women should make a comfortable home for the menfolk. Within the context of this dominant view about housework, the women are perceived as 'idle monkeys' and the most idle of all is Michelle. This is not because she wants to be idle but, rather, that illness has given her no choice. Annabel's reframing of the difficulty in this way allows Lily to find her voice and talk about the unfairness of illness and its consequences for her. Having heard her, the family agree with this new perspective and begin to talk together about how this problem might be solved. Reallocating some of the chores to the boys, asking for additional support from extended family members (identified on the genogram) and referring Lily to a young carers' group helps to reduce family tension while ensuring that the housework is done and to a standard that minimises Michelle's distress.

This example demonstrates the potential of the genogram to uncover hidden information in family life as well as documenting the more observable relationships.

Exercise

Think about a recent situation where the use of a genogram would have been helpful within your practice. Are there particular questions that might have helped you understand the situation more fully?

Timelines

Getting children to draw a timeline is another way of being able to elicit a lot of information in a very short space of time. All you need is a piece of paper and some felt-tip pens or crayons. The child is invited to draw a line across the page; it may be horizontal, vertical, diagonal or a line that makes a curl and meanders across the page. The next task is to ask the child or indeed the whole family to select an appropriate period of time. This may be as far back as the child remembers to the present day or maybe an agreed timescale starting at the point of diagnosis of serious illness. It is important that there is some space at the end of the line for future developments. Using a variety of coloured pens, the child can then mark any significant events along the timeline. This gives the practitioner an opportunity to gain some insight into what the child might or might not know about the illness but, perhaps more importantly, it establishes a basis for talking about and identifying strengths, resources and resilience within the family. Questions can be asked about how the family talked about the event, how they felt about it and if it was a problem, how it was resolved and by whom. A timeline can be particularly useful when children are talking about their current situation in a way that demonstrates that they feel totally overwhelmed and out of control. This is often indicated by their use of all-encompassing and sweeping phrases such as 'everything' or 'nothing'. Taking them back to a time when they faced a problem, which they managed to resolve, gives them a sense of mastery as well as a reminder of the life skills they possess.

Recalling an occasion of working with two young girls (both under ten) whose father had end-stage renal failure, a timeline was used to good effect. They had both given a great deal of information during genogram work about family relationships. In one session both started to do the timeline, which documented a number of significant life events they had experienced including moving house and changing schools several times as well as their father's illness. The elder child commented about how all the events that she was marking seemed to be very sad. She asked if it would be possible to have two parallel lines, a happy line and a sad line. In this way she created the opportunity for us to work collaboratively. Not unsurprisingly, her sister asked if she could do the same thing. Being able to acknowledge happiness made it easier for both girls to talk more freely about the profound sadness they had experienced at times. During the exercise they were enabled to name the things that had helped them through difficult times such as talking together, comforting each other when they were sad and finding a balance between sad and happy. On the happiness lines they were both able to mark out a number of things that they were looking forward to; these included the school play in which they were both performing and the long-anticipated family holiday. They both used the future sad timeline for marking the point 'Daddy dying'. Having written it down both girls began to cry. They were clearly overwhelmed by seeing it in print. Neither girl wanted to erase what had been written 'because it will happen' so we decided to cover the words with a brightly coloured Post-it® note. The future was still there but that did not mean that they had to look at it immediately nor would it have been either respectful or ethical to have used a position of power (being an adult) to get these two girls to talk about something that was clearly too emotionally difficult for them.

Body maps

In medical notes, healthcare professionals are used to seeing areas of pain, inflammation or skin rashes marked on a body map, but this can be a really useful tool when we are trying to get children's perspective of illness. The body map is a helpful way of getting a child to mark down which parts of mummy or daddy hurt or do not work as well as they might. This can help practitioners to understand what children know about anatomy, but also what they make of what they have been told.

It also creates an opportunity to hear the words that the children use to describe an illness, if indeed it has a name.

A slightly more sophisticated use of a body map may be to use it to explore feelings, not only for children to name how they feel but also where that feeling is located in their body. It is not unusual for children to highlight feet and hands as the place where they feel most anger and there is often a connection between this and the way that anger is played out, often through aggressive behaviours towards siblings or classmates.

One further use of body maps is to give them to children and let them add clothes to them, facial features or colour them in. While absorbed in this playful task, it can often be easier for children to talk without feeling that they are being 'interrogated' by an adult, with their every word being registered.

Giving information

There are some really useful resources that have been produced for supporting parents and practitioners in talking with children and helping them to understand difficult concepts; these include Stokes and Bailey (2000) and the Motor Neurone Disease Association's *Workbook for Children Aged Four to Ten* (2009). However, there are times when general principles have to be adapted as a way of increasing understanding. Flexibility is the key. For example, if children enjoy playing with construction toys, Lego® bricks can be used to begin to explain what cancer is. Here you could build a wall of bricks in one colour and insert a different coloured brick to represent the cancerous cells. Through discussions with the children, you can then begin to explain how the cancerous cells affect the body. However, it is good practice to invite the children to choose the colour of the bricks used, in order to avoid picking their favourite colour to represent the cancerous cells.

Vignette

Kusum was five years old when her father (Vijay) was diagnosed with cancer. In the 18 months that followed until her father died, she was helped to understand what was happening by a series of small conversations with her parents. Vijay worked in a garden centre and Kusum had always been exposed to talk about plants and crops. With this in mind, the cancer was initially described as being like a weed growing very close to a healthy plant and, in order to get rid of it, it needed to be removed (surgery). A little later, her father had to have chemotherapy and this was described in terms of when weeds grow back they sometimes need to be killed with chemicals. But then the disease recurred and Vijay had to have radiotherapy, which was likened to hoeing weeds to bring roots to the surface so that the sun could kill them. Finally, when all treatment options had been exhausted and it was clear that Vijay was going to die, the final part of the conversation was that sometimes weeds grow back, there is nothing you can do and they will kill the healthy plant. Kusum, who was now six, could comprehend what was happening to her father. Her parents rehearsed all these really difficult conversations beforehand so they could manage their own emotions and focus on reassuring their daughter that she was loved and always would be.

Observations of the vignette

Information about her father's illness and treatment was given to Kusum in small chunks. At each turning point in the illness, information was given in a way that she could understand and relate to. This approach meant that she was not overburdened with too much information too soon in her father's cancer journey.

Exploring thoughts, concerns, feelings
Storytelling

There are many story books available to help children address:

- significant life events
- thoughts and worries
- different feelings.

Often a story is based on the premise of facing up to adversity and overcoming it. Some books use cartoons, some have slightly ridiculous characters and approach serious subjects in an amusing way, some are therapeutic in intent and some are just a story. However, the caveat introduced in Chapter 2 needs to be re-emphasised. Story books dealing with dying and death need to be carefully selected and the content cautiously analysed before being shared with children. Therefore, when preparing to use a story book with children, always read it yourself before reading it with them. This enables you to familiarise yourself with the text and therefore begin to anticipate some of the possible questions or comments that the children may make. The key principles of good storytelling are provided in Box 5.1 below.

Earlier in the chapter we talked about establishing a rapport with children and part of this process involves finding out what interests them. It can be possible to use this information in a therapeutic way. For a number of children the impact of the *Harry Potter* series of books has been immense and a skilful practitioner who knows the content of the books can use some of the ideas to help gain a richer understanding of the lived experience of children who have a parent who is seriously ill. One example may be to get a child to draw the 'mirror of erised'. As 'erised' reversed is 'desire', it is the 'mirror of desire' and this creates a great opportunity for conversations between the child and the practitioner. More ideas about how the world of *Harry Potter* can be incorporated into practice can be obtained from Markell and Markell (2008).

What can be more fruitful, however, is making up stories in partnership with children or their making them up on their own. When given a box full of animal figures or play people, many children are keen to tell a story. Sometimes this may result in hugely imaginative plotlines that not only allow children just to have fun but also (more often) give you insights into their understanding and concerns. One child had parents who were convinced that he had no idea that his mother had MND. Their decision was to wait until her symptoms became more obvious before they talked about this with him. In play, the child selected a female figure holding a ski pole to represent the mother. During the story, he kept knocking the figure over with his finger. When asked why he was doing this, he replied, 'She's just like my mum—she holds onto the stick and pretends everything is okay but I know it's not.' His mum had tried very hard to hide her neurological symptoms and frequent stumbles by holding onto furniture, but nothing had escaped the eagle eye of her son. He expressed huge frustration with the skiing figure shouting out, 'You're so silly, you've stopped us going to see Grandma' (a holiday had just been cancelled). Hearing his story and watching him play, the parents realised he had a 'knowing' about what was happening that was unhelpful, and this prompted them to begin the difficult task of talking with him about the illness.

Another way of facilitating storytelling is to tape together several sheets of flip-chart paper, depending on the length of the child; ask the child to lie down on top of the paper and roughly draw around him or her (having first explained what you want to do and sought permission). Then invite the child to ascribe a name to the figure to tell a story. Because the figure is life-size, this can make for very powerful stories. But we can appreciate that flip-chart paper is not always to hand!

Box 5.1: Principles for good storytelling when the practitioner is telling a story

- Be enthusiastic.

- Be real – draw on your own experience to add colour and detail.

- Pay attention to the fit of the story for the listener – age, culture, gender.

- Observe your listener to gauge their responses and interest or lack of interest in the process.

- Give an outline rather than a full script – this enables the children to add detail.

- Be flexible in the way the story is told – make sure there are differences in emphasis and style of telling because this makes the story more interesting.

- Pay attention to voice – tone, volume, pace.

- Make sure the emotional tone in your voice corresponds with the emotion being expressed in the story – for example, happiness requires an upbeat tone.

- Language used should be appropriate for the children's age and cognitive development. When telling stories to small children, don't be afraid to invent silly names for characters or be playful with the story.

- Use metaphor where appropriate because this makes the story more memorable.

- Use the story to build on the children's resources and positive experiences as well as their coping strategies. The purpose of the story is to underscore their strength and resilience as well as to improve their understanding.

- The context of the story should not be too different from the children's own.

Language and comprehension

When giving a verbal account of their understanding of illness and treatment, even small children will use quite technical medical terms with a high degree of confidence: 'My mum has to go to the hospital every three weeks – that's where she has her chemo.' It is very easy to take this at face value and marvel at how well children can understand very complicated treatments. However, it is important to do a simple checking for congruence between language and understanding: 'Tell me a bit about chemo – what is it?' The answers can sometimes be surprising either because the children truly have got a very comprehensive understanding of what the treatment entails or, alternatively, because they are absolutely clueless, merely parroting back a phrase they have heard all the adults in the family use. If the latter, it gives the parent or practitioner an opportunity to explain what the treatment is, and it helps them to frame questions and explore feelings. It also means that myths and misunderstanding can be identified and addressed.

The use of metaphor

When conversations take place, the meaning of certain phrases that are used can be open to multiple interpretations. This is often the case when adults or children use analogy and metaphor. Metaphor is an indirect way of communicating ideas. It involves talking about something or using an image that parallels or represents something else. A good metaphor conveys complex thoughts and feelings and is never directly translatable. How can we recognise and use it to good effect?

Box 5.2 illustrates how attending to metaphor can help others get a different perspective on the illness experience and understand some thoughts and emotions that are attached to significant events (Barker 2008).

Box 5.2: An example of how metaphor can be used

A 14-year-old girl, Tracey, was talking about her mother's chemotherapy:

Tracey: Here we go again, the usual slide.

Practitioner: Slide?

Tracey: You know, chemo slide.

Practitioner: No, I don't know, tell me about chemo slide.

Tracey: Well, every three weeks my mum has to go and have chemo, she hates it, none of us look forward to it. And she gets really tired. Feels pretty rotten for about a week after she's had treatment. Then we have about a week when she is back to normal, we can go shopping together, have a bit of fun. And then it's back to thinking about the chemo again. It's like being on a slide; it's really hard work climbing all those steps but there's this wonderful moment when you're at the top, just about to slide down, you have a really great time and your heart just wants to go 'wheeee!' Then you get to the bottom and you get really sad because the fun is over. Then you realise you've got to climb the steps again.

Practitioner: Do you think climbing the steps is getting harder for your mum?

Tracey: Getting harder for all of us.

Practitioner: What about that wonderful feeling at the top? Is it worth climbing the steps for?

Tracey: Sometimes the slide down is so short and I do wonder if it's worth the effort. Not for me but for my mum.

Practitioner: What might happen if you stopped going up the slide?

Tracey: Maybe that's where the slide thing doesn't work; you can choose to stop going on a slide but you can't stop going and having chemo, can you?

Practitioner: Is this something you might want to talk to your mum about?

Tracey: No, if she wants to keep on crawling up the steps, maybe all I can do is follow up behind and give her a gentle shove of encouragement from time to time.

In this exchange, Tracey demonstrated a very sophisticated grasp of issues such as the impact of treatment on the whole family, respecting personal choice and doing the best you can. Reflecting back, Tracey's language helped her to talk in a way that a more direct approach might have inhibited.

Numerical rating scales

If healthcare professionals are assessing patients' pain, then there is a distinct possibility that they might use a numerical rating scale in order to assess the subjective view of their level of pain. A line will be marked in incremental points from 0 to 10 where 0 is no pain and 10 is the worst pain imaginable. In a similar way, rating scales can be used with children to ask any question related to feelings. So you might be able to produce, for example, a happy line, a sad line, a worry line or an excited line. Sometimes it is easier to talk about feelings in a more abstract way. If a child is creating a sad line, then maybe there will be more response if the question asked is 'What sort of things might be happening to make someone mark an 8 on the sad line?' rather than the more personal 'What might be happening to you that might make you mark an 8 on a sad line?' Young people in particular can often find it difficult to answer very direct questions. If creating an anger line, the scale can be adapted so that it is likened to a thermometer where the higher the score, the redder the colour, thus mirroring the more heated and explosive nature of anger for many children.

Never try to second-guess what children might consider to be an appropriate rating for any event. It is useful to start at the lower end of the scale and work upwards so that you address those things that are safer first. Watch and listen carefully for any verbal or non-verbal indicators that children are struggling to disclose their thoughts and feelings. This can be particularly true of powerful emotions such as worry or anger. If children have significant worries, the next step may be to help them share those worries with their parents or get their permission for you to discuss them on their behalf. Always collaborate with them to agree exactly what can be disclosed and the words that you might use. One nine-year-old boy, during the process of completing and discussing a worry line, divulged his fears that, if his mother was not around, his father would not be able to look after him and he would be put into foster care (a level 9 worry). He was almost paralysed with anxiety about this prospect because he had overheard his father saying he 'didn't know how he was going to manage when his wife was not around'. Initially he had been reluctant for his biggest worries to be disclosed to his parents but he did agree to have a family meeting where the worker would share his '6' worry – being teased at school. The supportive response from his parents gave him the confidence to ask me to go up the scale and tell them about his '9' worry. He was relieved to be able to share it and be completely reassured, by both parents, that whatever the future held he would always stay with his father. At that point he was unable to take the ultimate step and share his '10' worry about his mum dying and his dread of a life without her.

Paper, paint and crayons

Some of the easiest tools to access are a piece of paper and a pack of crayons or felt-tip pens. If you are working in either a school or a child's home, it is likely that these will be readily available. The request 'Draw me a picture of your family' can often give insights into emotional expression within the family, closeness or distance, or even relationships and family activities. When looking at the drawing together, curious questions can be asked very easily about differences between family members as well as what has changed and what has remained the same since illness came into their lives. An alternative strategy is to ask children to draw their family as animals and then discuss not only the reason for the choice but also the attributes that might be represented by each animal. The aim of drawing, as with any other intervention, is to help unlock thoughts and feelings that might otherwise remain hidden and unexpressed.

Taking the unlocking metaphor one stage further, children might be invited to draw a house with a large number of rooms (Crenshaw 2008). Beside this picture a key could be drawn and coloured in. Working on the premise that this is a magic key that can open the one room that contains something to make children happy, what would be found within the room? It should be made clear to children that this should not be a material possession. This type of exercise might be useful if children are exhibiting non-verbal cues that they are unhappy and that they want to be able to express the reasons for this to you in a way that does not just involve language.

In a more general way, it can often be helpful to get children to use paint or crayons to express either their feelings or how they see illness. One teenage girl helped to understand her anger (about her mother's illness) by depicting it as a hissing cobra. Another child, a boy of nine, was able to talk in detail about the impact of cancer on both himself and his family once he had drawn it as a large black shape with numerous spikes and barbed wire attached to it. The pain of his experience was belied by a neutral facial expression.

Practice point

The key to all drawing work is to get the children to interpret it for you rather than make assumptions for yourself.

Use of self as a resource – the 7 C's

Throughout the chapter a variety of interventions have been described. However, within these resources, the most important of all is the way in which we use ourselves. The 'fellow traveller' role is so important in helping children begin to navigate the alien landscape of parental terminal illness and the 7 C's as described here are key in this role:

- Confidence – to engage in work with children either directly or through their parents.

- Creativity – the capacity to think of ways to help children express themselves when use of language is difficult or as an alternative to talking.

- Curiosity – asking gentle questions that help understand children's experience.

- Congruence – working in a way that fits with the children and helps the practitioner to achieve a shared understanding of their perspective.

- Culture of the child – acknowledging and working with difference.

- Child focus – recognising and working with children in ways that accommodate their age, cognitive development and coping style.

- Concern – having genuine concern for the emotional well-being of the children. This should be at the centre of all the work that is done.

All these add up to improving the final 'C' – Communication.

Preparing to end sessions

As a patient's health status changes and/or deteriorates, it is probable that at some point a practitioner who has been working with the family may need to have an ending session. For children, the loss of a practitioner in whom they have confidence can be an additional layer of stress at a crucial time. Therefore, the timing of an ending should be carefully chosen. Where possible, it is helpful to flag up that the work is coming to an end and negotiate what will be done to bring it to a close. In the final session, it is useful to review what has been done together, to commend the characteristics the child has shown in facing difficulty and consider together how these life skills may be used in the future. Depending on the age of the child, this may be done in a conversational way or via cards, pictures or letters that the child and practitioner may be able to make for each other.

Continuing bonds

Quite intentionally, there has been a focus on practitioners working to encourage family communication, particularly with children. But what of the ill parent? When parents know they are dying, there is often a desire to leave something as a way of communicating with their child at a future time when they are no longer physically present. Some parents engage in writing letters for their children or producing treasure boxes for them. This work is emotionally laden and can be difficult for parents to do. For some, the act of putting pen to paper or thinking about the treasure to put in the box may be the first acknowledgement to themselves that they are dying. What might make this easier is if treasure boxes are turned into a family activity where the emphasis is on tips for living rather than messages from the dying. In a similar way, videos of day-to-day events are easier to do than a face-to-camera message to a child. In recent months Stephanie Barker has experimented with using small Dictaphone machines where a patient has been interviewed and encouraged to tell stories of family life. The tape can be downloaded as an audio file and saved to USB sticks so that all family members have their own copy. In this way, the hopes and dreams of the parent for the future of their children can be woven into the narrative. This type of intervention ties in with the often expressed existential concern that parents have about continuing to be present in the lives of their children even when they are dead.

Thinking about spirituality

The spiritual care of patients and their families is often associated with religion rather than broader ideas about belief and spirituality. However, it is important to consider the wider perspective and within this to consider the needs of the children living in the family. Cobb (2002), writing about spiritual care, suggests that 'in palliative care it is the beliefs not only of patients which are significant but also caregivers, an area seldom explored' (p.15). The term 'caregivers' would appear to be a catch-all for everyone associated with the patient, including children. Thinking about children's spiritual needs in the widest form is important when communicating with them. Questions about their identity are likely to be near the surface along with philosophical questions about life and death, especially for young people. Being able to explore the meaning of death helps children in their general meaning-making process. However, this is a subject that is rarely tackled. Professionals who erect communication barriers are unlikely to develop conversations that would encompass spiritual care. If a practitioner is anxious at the thought of using the words 'dying' and 'death', it is improbable that they will venture into the land of spirituality and belief. However, children are generally curious to know more in an attempt to answer meaningful questions.

Different professionals – what is their role in helping children communicate?

This section of the chapter will focus on the roles practitioners from different professions have in helping children to communicate, and also some of the specific issues that might get in the way of these exchanges.

Exercise

Before we begin to think about specific roles, briefly consider what your role is in helping children talk about serious illness and death.

Healthcare professionals

Healthcare professionals have a significant role in helping children communicate and find a voice. The nursing and medical teams are in a privileged position because of the knowledge they have about illnesses, treatments and trajectories. This information can be particularly helpful to children when they are trying to make some meaning from what is happening. Healthcare professionals can provide honest and timely information that will help the children develop their understanding and, potentially, coping strategies. The examples of the healthcare professionals involved with Miriam and John's parents in Chapter 4 illustrate the positive or negative effect they can have on the information-sharing process with children.

Healthcare professionals who work with terminally ill patients will be based within both hospital and community settings. Within their roles, the physical care of the patient has primacy and it could therefore be argued that it would not be within their remit to become involved with the children of patients. It could further be argued that the person who is dying is the patient, while the opposing argument is that, especially within palliative care, a holistic approach to care is taken and significant people in the ill person's life are also entitled to care and support. However, there continues to be some debate as to whether this holistic care always incorporates all family members or whether the emphasis remains with the patients and their partners. Notwithstanding this argument, the value of talking with children cannot be underestimated and healthcare professionals will have valuable information that can assist in the children's meaning-making process. As has been noted throughout the book, practitioner confidence can play a significant part in determining whether children are included in conversations. Lacking confidence or a belief in practice can prevent practitioners from contemplating this work, let alone having a go. This sometimes leads to their referring children on for 'specialist' help. While sometimes this is necessary, it can also have an unhelpful effect on the children. Another professional is being introduced into their lives, when in reality there will already be a number of new people entering their family. Talking to people who are familiar is regarded as being much more conducive and less inhibitory than being exposed to the possibility of needing to re-tell the story to a stranger.

Specialist practitioners

The specialist practitioners who are involved with a family will share some of the obstacles that their healthcare colleagues also encounter. A priority for specialist practitioners is the management of complex symptom control. Within this role, the needs of children within the family may not be seen as being their concern. However, their in-depth knowledge about symptoms could be invaluable in helping children understand a little more about what is happening to their parents and what care is being provided to them.

School personnel

When opportunities to discuss and explore what is happening become less prevalent for children within the home environment, other sources of support become invaluable. The classroom or school environment may become a safe venue for children to reflect on their experiences (Korn 1998). The school community can provide a reassuringly 'normal' environment where children can, for a short period, retreat to their pre-illness identities and get on with life. Conversely, school can also become a hostile, lonely environment where the dread of the future and others' lack of empathy for their predicament may turn the school setting into a strange and irrelevant place to be (Fearnley 2010). School attendance is a major feature of children's lives, and for the majority of children it is a cornerstone of their routine and sense of identity. Being part of the school environment is closely associated with 'fitting in' with peers; however, just as relationships with friends alter when a parent is dying, so can the relationship with school.

Teachers or other school personnel can contribute positively to help children explore what is happening and through this begin to make sense of the situation. They are key professionals for children both when they are living with a parent who is dying and following the death. They are the people who are likely to have most contact with the children and who are most familiar with them and their family. School staff, especially in the more familiar environment of infant and junior schools, could have been involved with the family for a number of years. Unlike the medical, nursing and social care staff who will have become involved with the family when the illness was diagnosed or as the patient's health deteriorated, the school personnel will typically have established a professional working relationship with the family and know the children well. Teachers are therefore in a privileged position to observe the children and note any variations in their behaviours that might be indicators as to how they are coping with the changes and challenges at home. Moreover, school personnel are likely to be the non-familial people that the children approach to talk to about their current situation.

However, Rowling (2003), writing about school communities, suggests that grief can be hidden within this community because 'it is unrecognized, unaccepted, or there is stigma attached' (p.152). All the staff within the school environment should have a responsibility towards the pastoral care of pupils, but sadly this is sometimes superseded by the overarching belief that education is the primary function. If teachers are under pressure to meet targets associated with the curriculum and are responsible for large class groups, the emotional and social needs of pupils will often be subsumed. Rowling (2003) goes on to observe that often it is difficult for teachers to cross the boundary from their professional role of informing students and having the answers to the role of not knowing what to say, which she suggests frequently occurs in grief support.

Moreover, many of the participants in Holland's (2001) research reported that they felt isolated and ignored by the school system, following the death of a parent. Holland observes that schools appeared not to have any systems in place for supporting children back into the system once the parent had died.

Rowling and Holland are predominantly discussing the systems within schools following a death and not during the pre-bereavement period. However, the findings from more recent research suggest that the pre-bereavement period is also a time when additional support from the school environment would be particularly helpful (Fearnley 2010). Therefore, for this to be facilitated, school staff need to be able to respond appropriately and have the confidence to know how to develop and nurture conversations. Having a school policy regarding supporting children concerned with dying and death is an essential starting point along with encouraging and enabling staff to access training on communicating with children.

However, for support to be put in place, the staff need to be aware of the home situation. It is not unusual, and totally understandable, for families to want to keep their affairs out of the public domain. On occasions, the enormity of what is happening within the family means that relevant information is not passed to school. It is therefore helpful if professionals involved with the family confirm that the school has been made aware of the situation. Parents may feel that they are protecting their children by not advising the school of the changes; however, generally, it is appropriate that the school does know. With this information they can monitor the children's behaviour and offer additional support if required. Conversely, if school staff are not made aware of what is happening, they may interpret the changes in behaviour, attendance and application as being a result of the children's inherent attitude to their education and not their current difficult family circumstances. When staff are not aware of what is happening, a great opportunity for external support is lost and, as a result, the children's well-being may not be as closely monitored as it should be.

Social care staff

Living with a parent who is dying places children at increased risk of not having all their needs fully met. Elements of their home life are likely to change to such an extent that aspects of their quality of life are jeopardised. Safeguarding and promoting the welfare of children is a role to which all professionals should adhere. This is highlighted by

Reith and Payne (2009) who attest that all professionals visiting the home should be alert to the possibility of child abuse or neglect, even when they are not themselves working with the children. While I am not suggesting that all children who are living with a terminally ill parent are at risk of significant harm, as defined by the Children Act 1989, I do believe that this community of children is at increased risk because of their circumstances. Parents who are struggling with all the pressures of terminal illness often find it difficult to provide the consistency of care that they had previously achieved. If the three domains of the *Framework for the Assessment of Children in Need and Their Families* (Department of Health 2000) are considered, it becomes apparent that elements within the domains will become fragile as the parent's illness progresses. The three domains are:

- parenting capacity
- child's developmental needs
- family and environmental factors.

The parenting capacity domain, for example, includes basic care, guidance and boundaries, and stability. As previous chapters have highlighted, boundaries and stability are both likely to be disrupted as illness progresses, and this can have a detrimental effect on how children see their worlds. The complete upheaval to family life, when a parent is dying, can be observed in some parenting patterns. Parenting styles can dramatically alter as the stress of the illness takes over. An example is parents' reactions to potentially benign behaviour, so their reaction to the children leaving their school bag in the kitchen may spark a huge argument. Prior to the illness this might not have occurred, and this consequently sends powerful messages to the children about how their lives are unfolding. If these uncharacteristic patterns of parenting become the norm, the children could be at risk of emotional neglect; however, this is a form of abuse that is often difficult to recognise. The difficulties in recognition are heightened if the children are 'invisible' within the system and are not recognised by the workers involved with the family.

Difficulties can again arise if the allocated social worker is for the patient and not the family. Miriam, whom we met in Chapter 4, experienced such problems. Her mother was allocated a social worker from the adult disability team but, because his role was to work with

Miriam's mother, he did not include the children in his assessment or in discussions about what was occurring.

The importance of the multi-disciplinary team

To date, different professions have been considered in isolation; however, the importance of multi-disciplinary and multi-agency working should not be underestimated. The *Working Together* guideline (Department for Children, Schools and Families 2010) 'sets out how organisations and individuals should work together to safeguard and promote the welfare of children and young people' (p.7). A first step in achieving this collaborative working is ensuring that all professionals working with terminally ill adults recognise that these patients may have children who are likely to be seriously affected by their parent's deteriorating health. Clear communication from the outset is important so that professionals from different disciplines and agencies are made aware that children are living in the family. This information should be received with the explicit expectation that all the professionals have a responsibility to acknowledge and recognise the children, and ensure that their well-being is being met. The analogy of the jigsaw is again relevant here because it is likely that different practitioners will have different pieces of information about the family. These small pieces, if joined together, may make a clearer picture about how the family functions and their communication styles. Moreover, when working across disciplines, the observations of the family and particularly the children can be especially beneficial. For example, a district nurse may see one element of the family that is different from the observations of the social worker or the GP. The children may present differently with different professionals who then only see one element. If workers are employed to work specifically with the children and build up a trusting relationship, their assessment is likely to be different from that of the worker who only sees them peripherally.

Recording systems

Linked closely to working together is the importance of good, clear documentation about the work undertaken or the observations made about the children within the family. There is a tendency for each profession to have its own recording system that documents the relevant points related to its purpose. So, for example, medical notes will include information about how the patients' medical symptoms are presenting and the treatment they have received. It is less likely that the notes will include equally comprehensive assessments of the patients' emotional and psychological state and unlikely that any detailed record of conversations about their children will be made. While the information about symptoms and treatment is absolutely vital, so too is the need to recognise the wider dynamics of the patient and their family. Parents who are worrying about telling their children that they are dying are likely to have significant emotional traumas that could be alleviated if workers spent some time exploring these important areas with them. This in turn could help them to feel emotionally and physically better. Having space within the recording system that specifically focuses on the issues of 'having conversations about the children in the family' would therefore not only prompt the initial conversation but also document what has been said and what actions are required.

Summary

This chapter has begun to explore some of the practical ways professionals can engage and begin to work with children who are living with a dying parent. We asserted at the beginning of the chapter that it has not been the intention to offer a 'cookbook' approach to working with children, rather a selection of tried and tested recipes that withstand a considerable amount of flexibility from the cook. The suggestions within this chapter are presented as practical interventions that can be added to the repertoire of the practitioner. The resources discussed include:

- genograms
- timelines
- storytelling
- art and craft.

However, the most valuable resource available is that of self. Having the confidence to be alongside children, not being afraid to acknowledge what is happening in their lives, and being able to talk about dying and death are such important assets. Our 'presence' with the children and being a fellow traveller on this journey is so vital. We talked about the 7 C's and how these are critical in the make-up of an effective practitioner.

The ideas presented in the chapter are intended to help more experienced practitioners and inexperienced workers like Lucy whom we have met in previous chapters. One way this can be achieved is through becoming 'playful' in our approach and allowing ourselves to enter into the children's worlds so that they have a voice and are included in conversations and information sharing. The resources offer the practitioner tools to engage in this playful approach.

Chapter 6

Children's Experiences of Different Death Circumstances

Stephanie Barker and Rachel Fearnley

Within this chapter we will continue to think about communicating with children when a parent's death is anticipated, but also to consider issues of communicating with children when a death is sudden. The chapter begins by looking at how bad news is given to children. The first section of the chapter provides a step-by-step guide to breaking bad news. This is intended as a guideline that should be adapted to meet the specific circumstances of each family. It is followed by a discussion about the preferred place of death and offers some suggestions that practitioners may want to consider when working with terminally ill patients. The focus then moves to sudden death and some of the implications for communicating with children in these circumstances.

Throughout the book issues around working with anticipated death have been explored where some degree of planning and preparation can be in place. However, what are the implications for practitioners who are faced with working with children where a death is unexpected? The dynamics are likely to be altered and different responses required. Consider class teachers who learn that the parent of one of their pupils has died suddenly following a heart attack. How can they respond to this situation? They will need to think about how the child will be integrated back into the school environment. Should they tell the class group and make the bereavement 'public' or should they try to 'carry on as normal'? They will need to consider how the child's behaviour may be affected, as well as a whole raft of other issues. What is in place to help teachers most effectively support these children and their families?

In circumstances of sudden death, different professionals are likely to be thrown into the fore. Paramedics, along with personnel from the other emergency services, may have contact with children when attending the scene. How they react and respond is imperative in the initial crisis. Likewise, staff teams within accident and emergency departments are also likely to experience such situations within their daily work. Many of the principles that have been discussed in previous chapters will be applicable here too. However, the significant difference is the 'instant' nature of the situation. The suddenness of the crisis brings an added complexity to the conversations that will need to be held with children. Some of these issues will begin to be explored in this chapter.

Exercise

Think about some of the different challenges children are likely to experience when faced with expected or unexpected death. What difference might there be with regards to:

- how they cope with the situation

- the support they might need

- what your role might be around the time of the different deaths?

Comment: an important note to make when thinking about these different situations is that, no matter what the circumstances are, the experience for each child will be unique to that individual. There are many factors that will affect how the children cope: their age, development, personality, family culture and, importantly, the extent to which they have been included throughout the experience.

Practice point

Whatever the circumstances of a death, there will often be a real need for the children to tell their story repeatedly. The telling and re-telling of events is important in helping them to begin to make sense of this terrible thing that has happened. As Frank (2009) observes, allowing people – children or adults – to tell their stories is an act of caring. Therefore, being comfortable hearing these stories is important, as is the recognition that they need to be repeated. However, it also needs to be recognised that at times children will opt not to talk about what has happened and will 'protect' themselves from any further pain by locking the memories away.

Within this chapter a distinction is being made between anticipated and sudden death. However, it needs to be recognised that an expected death – that is, where the patient has been ill for a period of time – may, in reality, be an unexpected death for children if they have not been included in conversations and, as such, are at the closed end of the communication continuum.

Breaking bad news

Throughout the book we have highlighted the importance of breaking significant conversations down into manageable chunks so that children can more easily process and assimilate the new information that they have been given. All these conversations are difficult for a parent to hold and they can be almost unbearable for the children to hear. Perhaps the hardest of all is when a parent knows that they are reaching the end of life and all family members begin to talk about the painful process of separation. If the parent has had a long-term condition, it is to be hoped that practitioners working within primary care will have had conversations about end of life care and advanced care planning over the preceding months. At an emotional level, these conversations are often easier to have when the patient is relatively well and a key skill is creating the opportunity for them to take place.

Breaking news is always emotionally draining so, if you know that you are going to be involved in having to do this work, it is important to be prepared. Being proactive in supporting parents for this difficult task can be very helpful in the long run. Get the parents to think about the environment and where the news will be broken; a familiar place is the most suitable because it helps children to feel safe and secure. This might be at home and at a time of their choosing, which relates back to the discussion in Chapter 2. Careful planning allows a parent to ensure that the children have comforting adults around them or, indeed, a comforting toy or teddy bear. The timing of such conversations is also important, and our advice to parents would be to steer clear of times in the day where there are chores or tasks to be done. Depending on the flow of family life, a good time might be after tea when homework has been done, the evening meal has been consumed and there is still time for the ritual settling children down for the night. All this allows the parents to be in control of the delivery and pacing of information. They can also create plenty of time to help their children to explore thoughts and feelings, to raise questions and, where possible, to have them answered. The very nature of end of life conversations means that some questions are either difficult to answer or, possibly, unanswerable.

Whether you are a professional talking to a patient and a partner or a parent talking to a child, being ill-informed or unable to answer questions only heightens the distress that bad news can bring. Doing some background work and having as much information as possible are prerequisites to breaking bad news, so spending some time looking at notes and talking to colleagues, or supporting parents to think about what to say, are essential starting points. Make sure you allow enough time to do this work and that there will be no interruptions or distractions, and do make sure that your mobile phone is switched off and the television or computer is not a distraction. The role of professionals is not necessarily to do direct work around breaking bad news to children, although at times they may be asked to. Rather, it is to support parents and help them rehearse what they might say and prepare for the responses and questions they may get. There is a significant role here for professionals to be proactive and encourage a family to talk about illness as early as possible, in bite-size chunks, as exemplified by the story of Kusum in Chapter 5.

Breaking bad news can be made a little easier if a framework for communication is used. There are several models of breaking bad news that can be followed (Brown and Bylund 2010) but all have the same key principles and practice that rely on sensitive communication, gently given at a slow pace that helps with assimilation. Taking a step-by-step approach, the guidelines in Box 6.1 may be helpful in relation to children.

Box 6.1: Guidelines for breaking bad news to children

1. Find out what the children already know. Questions such as 'What do you understand about your mum's illness?' can help you to understand what they know or, indeed, do not know. Sometimes it can be a real surprise and they give a response that demonstrates a full knowledge of not only what is wrong but also what the future may hold.

2. If children respond by saying, 'I don't know', then the next question might be, 'Would you like to know a little bit more about what is happening?' It is important to respect the children's wish not to receive information. However, there are times when they have to be told – for example, if death is imminent. If they do not want information, this might be a point to negotiate how much information they feel able to receive or to work out a signal whereby they can indicate when they have heard enough. Once, when explaining to two young boys about the treatment of cancer, the youngest one (aged five) was clearly fascinated and asked lots of questions, but there came a point when his older brother had become saturated with information and, rather than saying anything, he put his hands over both his ears, clearly signalling to the worker that she should stop. Respecting their differing needs, the worker gave two options: one was for her to continue the conversation with the younger brother in another room, and the other was for her to come back on another day and pick up the conversation with anyone who wanted to join in and talk. They both chose the latter option.

3. If the children want more information, this is the point at which a warning shot can be fired. This is a way of flagging up that something serious is about to be said. A typical example might be, 'We are worried because Daddy isn't getting any better.'

4. Here we get the most difficult part of all, imparting the news that 'Daddy has seen the doctor today who has told him that the treatment isn't working any more.' Before this conversation

starts, all adults involved should agree what message is to be conveyed, because in the face of emotional distress it is easy to become sidetracked by a strong emotional response such as anger or tears. For younger children the sentence alone may be enough information for this particular 'chunk'. However, for an older child or young person, it may be followed by 'and that means it is likely that Daddy will die very soon'. It can be very tempting at this point to offer general reassurance that everything will be all right. This is a natural and protective response, but ultimately it can be more helpful for children to express their fears and worries first, because this enables parents to be more specific in their responses. Also good, ethical practice dictates that reassurances about an ill parent's health do not offer false hope.

5. This is a key stage in the model of breaking bad news; it is the point at which the adult is responsive to what the children express either verbally or non-verbally. Part of the preparation of parents by the practitioner for breaking bad news should include a discussion of possible emotional responses from their children. These may range from a marked lack of interest, 'Can I have a yoghurt now?', to expressions of shock, disbelief, anger or overt sorrow. Parents are the experts when it comes to their children and they may already have an idea of how each child in the family will react. This helps the parents to tailor the way in which information is given. Given that this is a new situation for each family, then some thought about the reaction of the children can help the parents keep their own feelings in check (if only for the time being). The parents should also be prepared for their own emotional responses. If they become distressed during the breaking of bad news, they can be reassured beforehand that tears are okay and that being sad themselves may be a good way to model to their children that it is permissible to express emotion. Children often take their cues from adults about how they should behave.

6. Provide the opportunity for the children to ask questions and express any worries or concerns. Questions should be

answered as honestly as possible although some questions may
not be answerable.

7. Where appropriate, it might be opportune to summarise the
   information that has been given and then formulate a plan for
   what will happen next. For children this might be a specific
   plan or more general statements and reassurance that they are
   loved and will be cared for.

Sadly, all too often the first time an explicit conversation takes place
with children is when a parent is imminently dying and therefore the
capacity of professionals and parents to diminish the sorrow experienced
by the children is significantly reduced.

Preferred place of death

When talking with an adult about breaking bad news the questions
generated in step 6 may include consideration of a range of issues
about where the adult wants to die and what might help or hinder this
from happening. While dying at home is the preferred choice of many
patients, those who are parents may be concerned about the impact
that witnessing death at close quarters may have on their offspring. In
these circumstances, patients may decide to have end of life care in an
institution such as a hospice, hospital or specialist palliative care unit,
in order to try to protect their children from the burden of care and
responsibility as well as from high levels of psychological distress. These
worries may be influenced by the patients' own fears about dying and
it is important that healthcare professionals address these in the first
instance.

Dispelling myths about what happens when someone dies may help
a patient to decide that dying at home is a viable option. Often there
are fears about the symptoms at end of life such as pain, fatigue and
breathlessness, and the extent to which these can be controlled. Part
of the conversation will be an exploration of the patient's previous
experience of dying and death and it should also take account of any
cultural perspectives that may be important in order to meet the needs
of the individual patient. These may well have been identified through
genogram work at an earlier stage in the illness. Conversely, some
patients may choose to die at home and their end of life plan may

include a wish to keep life as normal as possible in a very abnormal situation. The balance is always between the normality of home life and the additional burdens that caring can impose on relationships.

What can be particularly difficult is when the patient and partner have differing views about end of life care and this may relate not only to the practicalities but also to the advisability of talking to the children about the imminence of the parent's death. This is congruent with research by MacPherson (2005) who highlighted that the dying partner's views and wishes tended to determine what information the children were given about the illness. Again, this is where sensitive and skilful communication on the part of the practitioner can be invaluable in addressing these issues and facilitating the parents to reach some consensus. This is likely to require the practitioner to be able to hold high levels of emotional distress, so it is important that clinicians have access to appropriate supervision in order to be able to reflect on practice. This issue is explored in more detail later in the chapter. Throughout all of this it is essential that the clinician brings the child's voice and perspective into the discussion. How easy would it be to silence children by ignoring their position within the family unit and not taking their ideas and concerns into account? Part of the equation is thinking not only of the 'here and now' but also the long-term consequences for the family in terms of relationships and family functioning. The value of having earlier conversations may now become apparent.

End of life care where death is expected

Over the past ten years attention has been turned to enhancing the quality of dying among the adult population. This is in part due to the high level of complaints received by hospitals relating to communication between healthcare professionals, patients and their carers at the end of life. For those patients who have a long-term or chronic condition where death would not be unexpected, we have seen, nationally, the introduction of the Gold Standards Framework (GSF), which is designed to ensure that practitioners work with patients and their families to think about advance planning for end of life care (Thomas 2011). This might include consideration of such practicalities as to where the patient wants to die and what might need to be put in place to enable this to happen – for example, extra nursing care, equipment or anticipatory prescribing for troublesome symptoms. Additionally, it provides a mechanism whereby multi-professional conversations can take place that address all the domains of good palliative care including physical, psychological, spiritual and social assessment. A key consideration for practitioners should be the impact of all these decisions not only on the psychological well-being of the patient but also on other family members, including children.

One crucial element of the GSF relates to the dying phase where we have seen many hospitals and community trusts implementing a care pathway to ensure that those who are dying receive optimum care. This model of care is often referred to as the Liverpool Care Pathway (LCP). One of the key principles of the LCP is clear communication with the dying patient and family members that the dying phase has been entered (Ellershaw and Murphy 2011). This is commonly viewed as the last 48 hours of life but it may be a longer or shorter period and is dependent on the identification of specific criteria that indicate a significant deterioration in the patient's condition.

Part of the documentation that accompanies the LCP is related to communicating the bad news that the patient will die soon, a conversation that should take place between clinicians and family members. We wonder how often it is documented that such conversations with children have been held or at the very least that it has been flagged up to other adult family members that this would be an appropriate thing to do.

This again is where it is essential to ensure that children participate as fully in end of life care as is practically reasonable. Clearly if a patient remains at home, it is easier to maintain normal routines wherever possible including going to school and attending after-school clubs and activities if this is what the children want. School plays a pivotal role in maintaining a sense of normality so it is important that heads of year or class teachers are kept up to date with any changes in the health and well-being of the children's parents. In many schools teaching assistants and pastoral care workers are allocated to be alongside children at this very difficult time so they can respond with some immediacy to high levels of emotional upset. Alternatively, many teachers will agree to some kind of sign or signal from children that allows them to remove themselves from class if they need to have some time quietly on their own. Additionally, how children are functioning or behaving in school can be a barometer of their level of adjustment or distress, and in this way reciprocal information and communication between teaching staff and parents become paramount.

Including children, even very small children, in the care of an ill parent can have significant ramifications for adjustment in bereavement. There is a fine balance between expecting children to have too much responsibility – for example, in the case of Lily whom we met in Chapter 5 – and excluding them from any involvement, which can lead to feelings of uselessness or isolation. Some children take great pride in being able to tell you that they are the only people who can plump daddy's pillows up in a way that makes him comfortable or prepare a drink just the way he likes it. Stephanie Barker will always remember a seven-year-old girl making it very clear that the nurses in the specialist palliative care unit could learn a trick or two from her! However, what we might need to remember is that caring for patients with complex needs can be quite scary.

Vignette

Xiu Li, a teenage girl who was suffering from panic attacks, disclosed that she was terrified whenever she was left alone with her father who, among other things, had had a stroke. When he slipped down in his chair, she was frightened to reposition him in case she hurt him. In one session she identified her mother as being expert and how useless she felt when she saw her mum helping her father. Together, using a piece of paper and a pencil, the continuum of 'helping Dad' was explored where expert was at one end and useless was at the other. Talking about the problems Xiu Li was encountering as concepts, rather than embodied in people, allowed her not only to reposition herself as *not* being useless but also to consider how she might get guidance from her mother that would enable her to move even closer to the 'expert' position.

Observations of the vignette

Xiu Li was understandably concerned about caring for her father, and the huge responsibility that accompanied this role. However, through time spent exploring 'helping dad', she was able to think, in a safe environment, about this role and begin to think about strategies that would help her develop some confidence to be more able to manage the situation.

Saying goodbye

For children, as with adults, it is important to have an opportunity to say goodbye.

Vignette

A young man, Joe, is imminently dying and being cared for at home by his partner Chris. He has two small children aged five and seven. Throughout his illness Joe has made it clear to you that he wants to be honest and truthful with his children. As a consequence you have assessed the children as being at the open end of the communication continuum (Chapter 4). One night Joe's condition deteriorates very markedly and by morning it is clear that he is likely to die before the day is over. When his children are awoken, it is immediately explained to them that Daddy is very poorly. The seven-year-old, Maisie, asks, 'Is Daddy going to die?'

Exercise

Think about the following questions:

1. As a professional, what might you have done previously that would have been helpful for the children today?

2. How could Chris respond to Joe's question?

3. Knowing that this is the day that Joe will probably die, what advice and support might you give to Chris in relation to the children?

4. How would doing this work make you feel?

Observations of the vignette

Joe knew that it was important to be truthful and honest with his children. Over a period of some months he had a number of small conversations with them that helped them to understand what was happening yet still remain hopeful. These could have been suggested and supported by a range of professionals. Joe was very clear with all other adult family members that they should also talk to the girls in a way that was honest, sensitive and loving, and this had been noted during genogram work on family beliefs and values. The pacing and timing of conversations would be key to helping the children understand the significance of his deteriorating condition. Given this preparation, Chris would be in a better position to respond to Maisie's question with a very gentle but very clear 'Yes, and it is likely that he will die today.' This exchange would be very difficult at an emotional level for all concerned but it would be so much easier because of all the previous conversations that had taken place. This was a confirmation of bad news rather than the telling of it. Both children could be given the choice of staying at home or going to school. If they chose to go to school, an opportunity should be created for them to be able to say 'goodbye'. If Joe died before the end of the school day, family members could meet the children in a quiet room at school with both class teachers present to break the sad news about their father. In this way, familiar adults from several areas of the children's life could simultaneously support them. A key message here, implicit rather than explicit, is that all the adults are talking and acting together. From the practitioner perspective, the most important interventions over the previous months would be to uphold the principle of truth telling, give some guidance about age-appropriate language and understanding in relation to illness, dying and death, and, most importantly, to commend brilliant parenting in the face of overwhelming personal anguish.

This is one example where the needs of a dying man and the needs of his children at the point of death had equal value. How easy might it have been for those two children to have been told that Daddy was too ill to see them, to keep quiet while they had their breakfast and got dressed, and then to be bundled off to school without the opportunity to say goodbye? The outcome would have been the same in that their father would still have died, but they would have been left with the memory of secrecy and silence rather than the reality of openness and participation.

This illustration, while appearing to be 'textbook perfect', does reflect a number of examples from practice that have been observed or participated in. What was additionally helpful was the way in which all the adults in the family collaborated to ensure the girls received the same type of communication approach from everybody. What can be much more problematic is where there are opposing views, particularly about what information, and in what detail, should be given to children. Therefore, it is important that practitioners explore not only what has been said to children about illness, treatment and prognosis but also if there are any barriers to communication within the internal family system. It may be that one parent holds core beliefs about the value of withholding information as a way of protecting their children. If so, this should be explored with both parents. The practitioner role in such circumstances is to balance support for well-intentioned ideas from the parent with helping them to understand what the impact of withholding information might be for the children, not only on their general well-being but also on trust within their family relationships.

Cultural difference

It is also important to take a broad view of cultural difference in communication patterns. Is openness a desired outcome? What might be the consequences of truth telling for the maintenance of hope within different cultures? Does the holding and/or sharing of information become the responsibility of males rather than females? If so, what might the implications be for female children having their voices heard? In an increasingly diverse society, it is important to be respectful of difference. An additional layer of complexity is added to communication when the first language of the practitioner is different from that of the patient and child.

Assumptions

Not that it would have made any difference to the outcome, but what gender did you assign to Chris in the exercise about Joe, Maisie and Chris? When we recall the story of Chandran in Chapter 4, what assumptions did he make about what was wrong with his mother? So, how do we know what meaning anyone ascribes to any given situation such as life-threatening illness? We might assume we know but, unless we ask and check it out, it remains a hypothesis. Consequently there is the potential for misinformation and misunderstanding, which in turn can give rise to emotional distress.

In order to manage assumptions about children's understanding about what is happening to their parents, a helpful stance to take is one of curiosity. Simple statements or questions such as, 'Tell me more about that' or 'What do you make of that?' can underpin a key function of practitioners – to aid family communication and understanding in the face of difficult and often confusing circumstances.

Visiting hospital

To a large extent we have focused on the experience of children when a parent dies at home. However, a significant number of patients still have end of life care in a hospital, hospice, specialist palliative care unit or nursing home. The challenge here is how children and the dying parent can be supported to maintain a connected relationship. Admission to any inpatient facility is usually because the patient either has a multiplicity of symptoms, all of which require a multi-professional approach to manage, or one symptom, which needs specialist intervention that cannot be provided by the primary healthcare team. By the very nature of the admission, the needs of the patient are likely to be prioritised over those of other family members. During the initial assessment phase, a pragmatic decision may be made to restrict or indeed dissuade children from visiting. This can be a very worrying time for the partner of the patient who may turn to professionals for guidance regarding the advisability of the children visiting. Factors to take into consideration include the age of the children and their level of cognitive functioning. Being given information in a clear way, with a full explanation of what is happening to their mum or dad, can enable older children to make an informed choice about visiting. For younger children a difficulty may be that institutional visiting times do not always fit well with the flow of school hours and out-of-hours activities. At a very unsettling time, it can be really important to maintain routines and this might include continuing with Brownies, Beavers or swimming club practice. Often, however, these important activities take place at a time that coincides with official visiting. The key question to ask would be about the possible flexibility of visiting patterns to accommodate children, particularly if the parent is dying. This might include asking about the possibility of children being able to stay overnight.

Hospital visiting can be difficult for adults because they do not always know what the rules are. Is it permissible to sit on the bed so that you can get physically closer to the dying patient? Is it acceptable to pull the curtains around the bed without asking a nurse so that you can have some privacy and the possibility of an undisturbed intimate moment? With these questions in mind, it is important to prepare children for the alien world of the hospital ward where some patients are very ill and keeping still and quiet is an expectation. Suggesting to the adults, who will be facilitating the children's visit, that they pack a bag containing a book, paper and colouring pencils (to make Mum or Dad a card), a Game Boy or an iPod means that the children will have a variety of things to do if their parent is unable to engage in a lot of conversation. In some hospital wards or hospices, there may be a family room where the children can go if they become unsettled.

For some children visiting a hospital can be an unnerving experience. It is therefore essential that they can make an informed choice, which is respected, and that they are listened to. If children have had a previous encounter with medical or nursing personnel that they associate with unpleasantness or possibly pain – for example, having had an injection – this may result in a phobia about clinics, health centres or hospital wards. Or maybe the emotional experience is just too hard. Under these circumstances, keeping the child connected to the ill parent during hospital admission requires some thought and preparation. Possible solutions might include the following:

- Getting the child to write notes or draw pictures that can be given by other family members to the ill parent.

- A two-way notebook whereby the child writes a note to the parent, the parent adds a response and sends it back. The notebook goes back and forth between home and hospital. This is only an option if the parent is well enough to write back.

- Using a mobile phone to text message. Again, this is dependent on mobile phones being allowed and the parent being able to engage with this as a two-way process.

- Some hospitals have the technology to enable patients to access the Internet. The same caveat as before would apply.

Unexpected death and the Intensive Treatment Unit

To date, we have largely been talking about the death of a parent as an anticipated and, we hope, a prepared-for event. However, for significant numbers of children the death of a parent can be both sudden and unexpected. If the parent is involved in a catastrophic event such as a road traffic collision and is admitted to an ITU, the scenario in relation to effective communication with children can be somewhat challenged (Vint 2005a). Given the nature of possible injuries such as contusions, swelling and broken limbs, it is quite likely that the parent will look very different from the last time they were seen by the children. Additionally, the patient may be attached to a range of machinery – for example, a cardiac monitor, intravenous infusion or possibly a ventilator. The inclination of adult family members to shield children from the experience of seeing a physically traumatised parent is understandable, but the reality is that children can be more frightened by what they imagine their parent will look like than the reality itself. The key here is clear information about what has happened and detailed preparation before children visit the ITU. Part of this preparation involves a description of what the parents as patients look like, what equipment they are attached to, what the function of each piece of equipment is and what noises the equipment is likely to make. If the parents are unconscious or attached to a ventilator, it can be helpful to give children an indication of what they themselves are still able to do and this includes talking to them, holding their hand or even giving them a kiss if they choose to. The body map described in the previous chapter is a really useful tool to help children understand what is happening before they visit. The positioning of any tubes or obvious bodily changes can be easily drawn. What we often forget is that some children already have knowledge of what happens in ITUs from watching television programmes, so the starting point for a sensitive conversation might be, 'What do you think ITUs are like?' This creates the opportunity to give as much information as they want or are able to hear, as well as correcting any misconceptions they may hold. However, there needs to be recognition, too, that sometimes the representation of these environments in television programmes and other media can be sensationalised for dramatic effect (Cox *et al.* 2004–2005).

When a patient is first admitted to an ITU, there may be a high degree of uncertainty about the outcome. However, as previously discussed, it is important that children are given the news about what has happened in a way that is sensitive to both their age and cognitive development. The principles of breaking bad news remain the same, but there is a strong likelihood that there will be several of these conversations with possibly very little space between them. During the phase of uncertainty, the skill can be in finding a balance between maintaining hope but also potentially preparing for the worst thing that can happen. Under these very difficult circumstances, the truthful answer to the 'Is my daddy going to die?' question may well be, 'I don't know, but hopefully the doctors and nurses will be able to give us some information soon that will help us all to understand what will happen.' The shock of what has happened may mean that the adult caregivers are emotionally overwhelmed and have little in the way of reserves to provide emotional support for their children. Proactive guidance on the part of the practitioner in helping the well parent rehearse what to say can be invaluable in these circumstances.

In some cases, when all treatment options have been exhausted, the point may be reached where either it is known that the patient will die very soon, perhaps in the next few hours, or possibly a decision needs to be made about switching off life-support systems. The decision to include children in witnessing end of life may be influenced by cultural considerations and the inherent knowledge a parent has about the emotional capacity of their children – whether it is more helpful for them to be present or to be with other adults away from the hospital. In these circumstances, relatives may well turn to professional caregivers for guidance and it is important that parents are given not only information but also clear signals that it is all right for children to be part of this family experience and that their presence in the ITU is not merely tolerated but actively supported (Vint 2005b).

Exercise

If you work in an ITU or an accident and emergency department, what was your answer to the question posed in the first exercise in Chapter 5 (see p.120) Within your team, think about all your policies and practice guidelines that incorporate communication in any way – do they explicitly include the children of patients?

Again, what is of paramount importance is that children are given a clear explanation of what is to happen and what their choices are. This allows them to be shored up to make their own decisions, something that is particularly important to young people who may want to play their own part in sharing family grief through both receiving and giving comfort. For small children, the decision to exclude them from end of life care may be to ensure that their physical needs for food, sleep and attention are met by family friends. This enables the parent and any older siblings to focus on being with and saying goodbye to the dying patient. If a decision is made to turn life-support systems off, it is important that all family members have the opportunity to say either a collective or a private goodbye to the dying person, and that they are encouraged to say anything they consider to be significant.

Exercise

Reflect on the reasons why family members and professionals might focus on meeting the physical and care needs of younger children. What might be the impact on their emotional well-being both now and in the future?

The unexpected death

When a parent has an unexpected event and dies suddenly – for example, following a heart attack or a cerebral bleed – the emotional impact can be enormous. In this context, breaking bad news cannot be done in carefully managed stages but has to be delivered in one phase. This means that there is no psychological preparation other than a brief warning shot that the children are about to hear something that is devastating. It is particularly important that the message the children are to receive is clear but delivered with great sensitivity. At times of great stress it is not uncommon for parents to use euphemistic language and doing so can only serve to increase confusion. A common example is to use phrases such as, 'We've lost your dad' and for small children, with a very literal frame of cognition, misinterpretation and misunderstanding can often be the consequence.

Not only does sudden and unexpected death complicate communication, it also means that there is no opportunity for any family member to say goodbye. The long-term consequences of this can be manifold. In bereavement, children can sometimes choose to ruminate on the last dialogue they had with the deceased parent. What if the last conversation was a row or a sharp volley of words, a not uncommon scenario between parents and their adolescent children? These unresolved exchanges may give rise to feelings of sadness compounded by anger and guilt – in short, high levels of expressed or internally experienced emotion.

Any unexpected death requires additional formalities to be completed. A coroner's inquest usually takes place a few months after the death has occurred and some families exist in emotional limbo until the cause of death has been officially ratified. This can make it very difficult for parents to give definitive answers to any questions children might have. Practitioners who remain involved with such a family need to be aware of these additional complexities that can compound family grief and, more importantly, interrupt family communication. High levels of distress can be picked up through the context of GP consultations or school life, but the converse is also true (see Chapter 5).

Murder and suicide

As with unexpected death, murder or suicide creates a more complicated context of communication with children. Overwhelming shock and distress are often the most prevalent emotions in the first instance. Depending on the particular circumstances surrounding the death, there may be additional feelings of shame or guilt. Furthermore, the death may generate unwelcome media interest. Surviving parents may find it difficult themselves to understand and accommodate the reality of the mode of death and, in such circumstances, making sense of what has happened and relaying this to children can seem an impossible task. In the case of suicide, the parent may choose to keep the exact nature of the death a secret from the children. The long-term consequences here are that the parent and children have no common story to share about the death and this can get in the way of the family grief. The implications for communication with children are clear.

If the death is a result of murder and depending on the circumstances, the safety of all family members may be a priority for all professionals involved. Any resulting trauma from either witnessing the event or hearing about details of the death is most likely to require psychotherapeutic intervention from specialist practitioners.

The role of practitioners in sudden death

Whether the death of a parent occurs at home or in hospital, is sudden or expected, the family is likely to come into contact with a broad range of health and social care practitioners. In this new and probably frightening life (death) event, it is almost inevitable that support and guidance may be sought from the 'experts' with whom the family comes into contact. What can add to the upset at this very difficult time is being given conflicting opinions from professionals about what is and is not helpful in relation to communication with children. So the key points for practitioners, whether they be teachers, nurses, doctors, social workers, victim support workers, emergency service personnel or funeral directors (to name but a few) are as follows:

- Always work in partnership with parents, respecting their culture and core beliefs. If the adults have not shared information about the death with other professionals involved in the life of their children – for example, teachers and classroom assistants   they should be encouraged to do so.

- Truth, however painful, is more helpful in the long term than well-intentioned silence or lies.

- Be aware of your own experience, both personal and professional, and the influence that this might have on giving advice and guidance of an emotional nature. Our own prejudices about what is 'right' in relation to truth telling can influence how we act and respond. What the evidence tells us is that, while there may not be a definitive 'right or wrong', there is certainly a more helpful way of supporting parents and their children.

- If in doubt, 'I don't know' is better than giving advice based on gut instinct rather than knowledge.

- Do not be formulaic in the advice you give. Adapt what you know to fit the particular circumstances – one size does not fit all.

- Children are often more emotionally resilient than we give them credit for. This is particularly so if supported by adults who can provide either physical and or emotional comfort and can help them make sense of a situation that at times seems incomprehensible. Health, social and educational practitioners can all have a place in recognising and facilitating this.

Considerations following the death

It is important to have some conversations before the death about the extent of the children's involvement once the parent has died. This allows for some forward planning but also gives children the opportunity to think about potential scenarios and begin forming these in the narratives of their lives. These conversations need to include not only the children but also their parents so that everyone has the opportunity to explore issues and develop a common understanding.

The debate about whether children should be allowed to view the body or attend their parent's funeral is likely to be high on the agenda. Adults who try to protect children from the messy, unpredictable nature of adult life are likely to extol the virtues of exclusion. Their argument would probably follow the lines that children are too young to understand and should not witness the potential outpouring of grief at the ceremony. Moreover, they would state that funerals are 'no place' for children who may not behave appropriately in such circumstances. The alternative argument, presented by more liberal-minded folk, would be that adults should be proactive in encouraging children to have choice about being involved. Within this argument, the importance of choice would be advocated along with the benefits of participating in rituals that are so important in celebrating the life of the deceased. Children's attendance at funerals will be explored in more detail shortly, but first the subject of whether children should view the body will be briefly discussed.

Viewing the body

Conversations with funeral directors from across the United Kingdom suggest that there are some consistent observations made about children viewing the body of a parent. A striking commentary is that adults will typically arrange to visit the chapel of rest during school hours. Whether this is a practical solution to allow for child care or a more prohibitive action to exclude the children is open to debate. However, examples of when children do view the body would suggest that typically they cope better than the adults anticipate.

There may of course be occasions when it would be wise to be cautious about the appropriateness of children viewing the body. If the cause of death was violent or the body severely disfigured, there are often concerns that they should not see the body. However, Dyregrov and Dyregrov (2005), writing particularly about suicide, suggest that 'when an adult can view a dead body, there is no reason to exclude a child' (p.210). However, they go on to caution that it is imperative that the children are properly prepared for the experience.

A caveat that must be included here is about children having choice. If they are offered the opportunity to view the body but choose not to, this must be respected. However, the important factor here is that they have been given choice and have some control over their lives. Second, it is important to recognise that they may initially agree to attend the viewing but then decide that they do not want to be included. Being in a position to make an informed choice about whether or not they want to view the body is greatly determined by having sufficient age-appropriate information. The chapel of rest will be an alien place for children and they will not know what to expect. Anticipating some of their questions and offering reassuring answers will help them to make an informed choice about viewing the body. Here the role of funeral directors is imperative. There are two important roles they can assume. The first is to discuss with the family about whether or not to include the children. The family may not have considered the possibility that the children should be involved and therefore an informed discussion with the funeral director can be particularly helpful. Second, funeral directors can help prepare children for visits to the chapel of rest. They can talk to them about what they will see, what the room will be like, what the body will look like and, importantly, give them permission to leave the room at any time.

Vignette

Sally's mother died two weeks after being admitted to the specialist palliative care unit. Following her death, Sally's father and maternal grandmother began making the funeral arrangements. They arranged to meet with the funeral director mid-morning when Sally was at school. During this meeting the funeral director asked about arrangements for viewing the body and explained that things would be put in place to accommodate Sally at the chapel of rest. Her father and grandmother informed him that they felt it was better if Sally was not involved because she was 'too young' to understand what was happening. The funeral director gently acknowledged what they were saying but also offered personal observations of previous similar family circumstances. He talked about the value of including children, even quite young ones, in the rituals of death and how this was generally seen as being helpful in their mourning. Initially Sally's father remained reticent about allowing her to visit the chapel of rest and made a number of telephone calls to the funeral director before agreeing that she could be given the choice. It was agreed that she and her father would meet the funeral director and everything would be explained to her. This happened and, although Sally was naturally anxious about seeing her mother, she also made it clear that she wanted to say goodbye to her before the funeral. Her initial anxieties quickly left her when she went to view her mother and chatted about her week at school and how the teacher had been 'extra kind' to her. That evening, Sally told her father that she was really pleased that she had seen her mummy because now she knew where she was and was reassured that she still looked the same.

Observations of the vignette

Sally's father and grandmother initially expressed concerns about her age and level of understanding in relation to being involved with the funeral rituals. However, through careful planning, Sally was given the opportunity to make an informed choice about viewing her mother's body. Because this was handled with sensitivity and care, it became a positive experience that helped Sally and offered her some understanding of her mother's death.

Attending the funeral

Giving children choice about going to the chapel of rest is important, as is the option to attend and participate in the funeral. Holland (2001) notes that, following the death of a parent, one of the problems facing the surviving parent is whether or not to include the children in rituals including attendance at the funeral. Furthermore, he highlights that such decisions need to be made quickly when inevitably the family is upset and in a state of shock and turmoil. Therefore, it is important whenever possible that such conversations are held prior to the death.

Factors that may influence an adult's decision whether or not to include the children are:

- the age of the child

- the family's culture and history

- societal or local community influences

- external influences – family and friends offering their opinion

- the media – did the child from the favourite soap opera attend the fictional funeral?

Whatever the factors are that influence the individual's decision, research consistently suggests that children who have attended the funeral (or who have had a choice in deciding whether or not to attend) have benefited from the experience (Holland 2001; Holland 2004; Riches and Dawson 2000). In Holland's (2004) research, 36 per cent of children who had attended their parent's funeral expressed the view that it had been a positive experience, while 35 per cent of children who did not attend the funeral said that they had some regrets about not attending.

Who will support me?

As this chapter concludes, there is a move in emphasis away from the needs of children to support for the practitioner. Throughout the book the focus has been on practitioners ensuring best practice for children and their families. However, it is also really important that our needs are also acknowledged and taken into consideration. As has been noted throughout the book, working with children when a parent is at the end of life is an emotionally complex role. When the work is undertaken sensitively and with due regard for all the competing demands placed on the children, the strain on the practitioner can be potentially severe. Within this work, there is a risk that emotions and unresolved conflicts are heightened and thus have an impact on both the personal and professional identity. Being a fellow traveller with children who are experiencing such huge and traumatic events in their lives is inevitably stressful. Therefore, it is important that appropriate and adequate support is routinely available. This is true whether you are an experienced practitioner or a newly qualified worker such as Lucy whom we first met in Chapter 2.

Exercise

Spend some time reflecting on the following bullet points:

- Can you recognise stress in yourself? How and where do these feelings manifest themselves and how do you recognise them?
- What strategies do you have to manage stress?
- What supervision do you have in place?

Comments: How easy did you find the exercise? Did it raise questions or ideas that need to be explored further? How easy was it to identify the strategies you have for managing stress? Some people have robust mechanisms in place for combating stress associated with work – for example, making time each day to get away, briefly, from their desk or having five minutes' quiet, reflective time. These brief times away from the hustle and bustle of work are important and should be seen as a priority not a luxury. Being able to recognise and manage stress is important; however, as workers we are often very poor at 'protecting' ourselves and see stress as a sign of weakness or failure.

Supervision is a vital component in helping to manage stress and it should be a fundamental right for all practitioners. Howe (2008), writing about the emotionally intelligent social worker, suggests that:

> supervision and consultation are essential if practitioners are to remain self-aware and emotionally attuned…supervision contains significant elements of self-reflection and analysis in which social workers think about how clients are affecting them emotionally and how they emotionally affect clients. (p.186)

If you are unable to access regular supervision, are there ways that it could be developed? Could one-to-one, peer or group supervision be organised within your team? If you do not work within a team, would it be possible to access support from another team? Could cluster groups be developed locally or regionally whereby practitioners meet regularly to discuss practice and offer mutual support?

It is not our intention to provide any in-depth suggestions for stress management – there are many books and resources available today that fulfil that role. However, we do feel that it is important that such an important issue is raised and acknowledged. Being confident and competent in communicating with children whose parents are dying is greatly enhanced when appropriate support is in place for the worker.

Summary

This chapter has moved away from focusing primarily on anticipated deaths so as to incorporate some discussion about situations where a death is sudden. Within this we have started to consider some of the implications for practitioners when communicating with children about the sudden and unexpected death of their parent. Many of the principles that have been extolled throughout the book remain the same. However, some factors add to the complexity of these conversations. Within these circumstances, there are no opportunities to gently prepare the children for what is about to be told to them. In some situations, there is a period between the medical event and the death, where the medical team is working to save the patient's life. Wright (1991), describing his research into sudden death, suggests that people in such liminal periods describe this time as 'torment'. The uncertainty of what is happening and the conflicting struggle between hope and fear will potentially be huge. In these circumstances, practitioners need to think carefully about how they are able to communicate with the relatives, especially the children, and what should be communicated. Some key considerations include:

- providing clear, sensitive information

- giving the children informed choice about their involvement

- thinking about which other familiar adults, in the children's lives, could offer ongoing support into the bereavement period.

The chapter concludes with a discussion about support for practitioners. It should never be underestimated how emotional this work is and the detrimental effect it can have on workers. Therefore, receiving appropriate and regular support is really important in helping to maintain a positive perspective about the work and provide the most effective support to children and their families. Some practitioners fear that asking for support is a sign of weakness when actually the opposite is true. Being sufficiently reflexive and self-aware to recognise that working in isolation is not helpful or good practice demonstrates a high level of competence and confidence.

Conclusion

The mantra 'communication, communication, communication' has been ever-present throughout the book and the virtues of professionals embracing the theme have been constantly extolled. The journey has explored differing communication themes. However, whichever route we have taken, there have been similar vistas along the way and the same destination, the death of a parent, has always been reached.

The unpredictable world of parental terminal illness often leaves children feeling isolated and excluded. The enormity of the family crisis pervades every aspect of their lives and has the potential to disrupt the very core of their being. The stress of living with a parent who has received a terminal diagnosis is difficult enough to cope with, but, when this is compounded with a wall of silence, the enormity of the situation is manifold. Similarly, the parents are catapulted into an unplanned and uncertain situation that encroaches on all that was previously safe and known. It is hardly surprising therefore that parents often struggle to talk with their children about what is happening. Sometimes the fear of talking to them is the precursor to this wall of silence while on other occasions it is the belief that they do not need to know. However, what has been stressed is that, no matter how well the parents try to conceal what is happening, the children will be aware that something is occurring within their family. Within these circumstances, professionals working with the family need to intervene and help generate some conversations that will facilitate the children's understanding and help in the meaning-making process so that they can have some control over the situation.

However, as we have seen, professionals are not immune to feelings of uncertainty and apprehension when involved in talking to children about dying and death. A 'professional impotence' is not uncommon – whether this is due to the emotional weight of the subject matter, the desire to protect children or the fear of entering into dialogue. However, what has been acknowledged is that practitioners from all professions are pivotal in encouraging these conversations, whether this is directly with the children or indirectly with their parents.

The choice of language is really important when communicating with this population of children. This includes selecting words that are non-euphemistic in nature, that are simple and that are age appropriate. The employment of euphemistic language has been explored and it has been speculated whether such language is chosen, by professionals, as a shield to protect them from the messy harshness of death. Being afraid to use the words 'dying' and 'death' inhibits conversations and this fear is a barrier to becoming an effective resource. The tone of voice adopted is important as is the pacing within conversations. Offering small 'chunks' of information is especially helpful and assists children in the absorption of the facts and consequently in their meaning-making process. Also, because the information that is being shared is incredibly sensitive and potentially life changing, it is critical that during conversations with children professionals take time to clarify that the children have understood what has been said to them.

There are many resources available that can be incorporated into the practitioner's toolkit. Some of these have been discussed including the communication continuum, which is a practical idea that has been developed through my own research. The continuum can be used when making an assessment of where children are in relation to their involvement in discussions and information sharing about their parent's illness, and also practically when working with children. In Chapter 5, we introduced a number of different resources that can be easily adapted for working with children whose parents are at the end of life. Each of the resources can be used 'playfully' with children to help in the engagement process and to facilitate communication. However, when using these resources, the most valuable resource of all is that of self. Being able to enter the world of the children and to become a fellow traveller who is genuinely by their side for part of the journey is key. Part of this ability is about having good communication skills. Effective communicators are sensitive in their approach and moreover display compassion. In the context of this book, being sensitive includes recognising cues from the children and responding appropriately. Being cognisant that they will not necessarily want to engage in a conversation about their parent's imminent death should be respected and worked with.

Practitioners from a wide array of professions are likely, within their working lives, to be involved with children whose parents are dying. In some situations, it will be an anticipated death, the result of a life-threatening illness that has become terminal. In others, it will be the result of a sudden crisis of health or some kind of trauma. Whatever the circumstances surrounding the dying and death, in order to be most effective in their practice, professionals need to be confident and competent in communicating with the children and thus supporting them.

A key message for practice is that, if we are genuinely providing holistic palliative care, then a wider perspective than just the patient has to be adopted. The family needs to be included but, more specifically, the children need to be involved in what is happening within their family. Life-limiting illness does not only affect the patient: it seeps into all family life, affecting each member in different ways, and often into the wider community too. Children are at risk of being marginalised and ignored during this period and, as a consequence, we as professionals are at risk of letting down vulnerable service users. It is therefore imperative that holistic care does take a family perspective and, central to this, that the voices of the children are encouraged to be heard.

In Chapter 1 I introduced the '3 P's': policy makers, professionals and parents. Professionals have a dual role in encouraging conversations with children about parental terminal illness. First, there is the primary function of, where necessary, initiating the conversations either directly with the children or with their parents, with the purpose of encouraging them to talk to their children. Second, I believe there is a wider scope to their function. Taking the debate to policy makers, and having this included in the political landscape, is really necessary if children who are living with a parent who is dying are to become visible. If there is any hope of moving away from the situation that was so persuasively described by Silverman (2000) at the beginning of the book, we as professionals need to influence policy, which in turn will influence practice. These children need, at the very least, to be listened to and engaged in shared communication. Having adequate information at their disposal will allow them to make informed decisions about the reality of their experience and, through this, to have some control in the journey they are travelling with their parents. When we are silent, the children are silenced and we have failed in our responsibilities. When we are silent, another 'Bernard' is at risk of being ignored by all the adults around him.

References

Barker, S. (2008) 'Unlocking the box: Talking with families about death and dying.' *Primary Care Review (Summer)*, 264–265.

Barnes, J., Kroll, L., Lee, J., Jones, A. and Stein, A. (1998) 'Communicating about parental illness with children who have learning disabilities and behavioural problems: Three case studies.' *Child: Care, Health and Development 24*, 6, 441–456.

Baym, N.K. (2010) *Personal Connections in the Digital Age: Digital Media and Society Series.* Cambridge: Polity Press.

Beale, E.A., Sivesind, D. and Bruera, E. (2004) 'Parents dying of cancer and their children.' *Palliative and Supportive Care 2*, 387–393.

Brookes, L. (2006) *The Story of Childhood: Growing Up in Modern Britain.* London: Bloomsbury Publishing.

Brown, R. and Bylund, C.L. (2010) 'Theoretical Models of Communication Skills Training.' In D.W. Kissane, B.D. Bultz, P.M. Butow and I.G. Finlay (eds) *Handbook of Communication in Oncology and Palliative Care.* Oxford: Oxford University Press.

Buckman, R. (1992) *How to Break Bad News: A Guide for Health Care Professionals.* Baltimore, MD: The Johns Hopkins University Press.

Cattanach, A. (2007) *Narrative Approaches in Play with Children.* London: Jessica Kingsley Publishers.

Children Act (1989) London: HSMO. Available at www.legislation.gov.uk/ukpga/1989/41/contents, accessed on 30 October 2011.

Chowns, G. (2005) 'Swampy Ground: Brief Interventions with Families Before Bereavement.' In B. Monroe and F. Kraus (eds) *Brief Interventions with Bereaved Children.* Oxford: Oxford University Press.

Chowns, G. (2008) '"No, you don't know how we feel": Groupwork with children facing parental loss.' *Groupwork 18*, 1, 14–37.

Christ, G.H. (2000a) *Healing Children's Grief: Surviving a Parent's Death from Cancer.* Oxford: Oxford University Press.

Christ, G.H. (2000b) 'Impact of development on children's mourning.' *Cancer Practice 8*, 2, 72–81.

Christ, G.H. and Christ, A.E. (2006) 'Current approaches to helping children cope with a parent's terminal illness.' *CA: A Cancer Journal for Clinicians 56*, 4, 197–212.

Christ, G.H., Siegel, K. and Sperber, D. (1994) 'Impact of parental terminal cancer on adolescents.' *American Journal of Orthopsychiatry 64*, 4, 604–613.

Christensen, P. and James, A. (2001) *Research with Children: Perspectives and Practices.* London: Routledge.

Cobb, M. (2002) *The Dying Soul: Spiritual Care at the End of Life.* Buckingham: Open University Press.

Collins (1995) *Collins English Dictionary.* Aylesbury: HarperCollins Publishers.

Cox, M., Garrett, E. and Graham, J.A. (2004–2005) 'Death in Disney films: Implications for children's understanding of death.' *Omega 50*, 4, 267–280.

Crenshaw, D.A. (2008) 'The Magic Key.' In L. Lowenstein (ed.) *Assessment and Treatment Activities for Children, Adolescents and Families.* Toronto: Champion Press.

Daily Telegraph, The (2010) 'Kisses, rugby, now and then a sunflower: Dying wife leaves husband a wish list for their young boys.' 1 October, p.9.

DasGupta, S., Irvine, C. and Spiegel, M. (2009) 'The Possibilities of Narrative Palliative Care Medicine: "Giving Sorrow Words".' In Y. Gunaratnam and D. Oliviere (eds) *Narrative and Stories in Health Care: Illness, Dying, and Bereavement.* Oxford: Oxford University Press.

Department for Children, Schools and Families (DCSF) (2010) *Working Together to Safeguard Children: A Guide to Inter-agency Working to Safeguard and Promote the Welfare of Children.* Nottingham: DCSF Publications.

Department for Education and Skills (2003) *Every Child Matters.* London: The Stationery Office.

Department of Health (2000) *Framework for the Assessment of Children in Need and Their Families.* London: The Stationery Office.

Doka, K.J. (ed.) (1989) *Disenfranchised Grief: Recognizing Hidden Sorrow.* New York, NY: Lexington Books.

Dunning, S. (2006) 'As a young child's parent dies: Conceptualizing and constructing preventive interventions.' *Clinical Social Work Journal 34,* 4, 499–514.

Dyregrov, K. and Dyregrov, A. (2005) 'Helping the Family Following Suicide.' In B. Monroe and F. Kraus (eds) *Brief Interventions with Bereaved Children.* Oxford: Oxford University Press.

Ellershaw, J. and Murphy, D. (2011) 'What is the Liverpool Care Pathway for the Dying Patient (LCP)?' In J. Ellershaw and S. Wilkinson (eds) *Care of the Dying: A Pathway to Excellence.* Oxford: Oxford University Press.

Elmberger, E., Bolund, C. and Lutzen, K. (2005) 'Experience of dealing with moral responsibility as a mother with cancer.' *Nursing Ethics 12,* 3, 253–262.

Erikson, E.H. (1963) *Childhood and Society.* New York, NY: Norton.

Fearnley, R. (2010) 'A lonely place to be: Children's experiences of living with a parent who is dying.' Unpublished PhD thesis, University of Derby.

Frank, A.W. (2009) 'The Necessity and Dangers of Illness Narratives, Especially at the End of Life.' In Y. Gunaratnam and D. Oliviere (eds) *Narratives and Stories in Health Care: Illness, Dying and Bereavement.* Oxford: Oxford University Press.

Freeman, J., Epston, D. and Lobovits, D. (1997) *Playful Approaches to Serious Problems.* New York, NY: W.W. Norton & Company Limited.

Glaser, B.G. and Strauss, A. (1980) *Awareness of Dying.* Chicago, IL: Aldine.

Goodwin, J. and Horowitz, R. (2002) 'Introduction: The methodological strengths and dilemmas of qualitative sociology.' *Qualitative Sociology 25,* 1, 33–47.

Heaven, C. and Maguire, P. (2005) 'Communication Issues.' In M. Lloyd-Williams (ed.) *Psychosocial Issues in Palliative Care.* Oxford: Oxford University Press.

Holland, J. (2001) *Understanding Children's Experiences of Parental Bereavement.* London: Jessica Kingsley Publishers.

Holland, J. (2004) 'Should children attend their parent's funerals?' *Pastoral Care 22,* 1, 10–14.

Howe, D. (2008) *The Emotionally Intelligent Social Worker.* Basingstoke: Palgrave Macmillan.

Hunt, K.F. (2006) 'Do you know Harry Potter? Well he's an orphan: Every bereaved child matters.' *Journal of Pastoral Care in Education 24,* 2, 39–44.

Jones, P. (2009) *Rethinking Childhood: Attitudes in Contemporary Society.* London: Continuum International Publishing Group.

Kavanaugh, R.E. (1972) *Facing Death.* Baltimore, MD: Penguin Books Inc.

Kennedy, C., McIntyre, R., Worth, A. and Hogg, R. (2008) 'Supporting children and families facing the death of a parent: Part 2.' *International Journal of Palliative Nursing 14,* 5, 230–237.

Korn, C. (1998) 'How young children make sense of their life stories.' *Early Childhood Education Journal 25,* 4, 223–228.

Lakhani, M. (2011) 'Nothing about me without me.' Paper presented to the Subscriber Forum, The National Council for Palliative Care, 16 March, Westminster, London.

Lefevre, M. (2010) *Communicating with Children and Young People: Making a Difference.* Bristol: Policy Press.

Lewandowski, L.A. (1996) 'A parent has cancer: Needs and responses of children.' *Pediatric Nursing 22,* 6, 518–521.

Lewis, F.M. (1990) 'Strengthening family supports: Cancer and the family.' *Cancer 65,* 3, Supplement, 752–759.

Lord Laming (2003) *House of Commons Health Committee, The Victoria Climbié Inquiry Report: Sixth Report of Session 2002–2003.* London: The Stationery Office.

McGoldrick, M., Gerson, R. and Petry, S. (2008) *Genograms: Assessment and Intervention.* London: Norton Professional Books.

McKee, D. (1980) *Not Now, Bernard.* London: Random House Children's Books.

MacPherson, C. (2005) 'Telling children their ill parent is dying: A study of the factors influencing the well parent.' *Mortality 10*, 2, 113–126.

Markell, K.A. and Markell, M.A. (2008) *The Children Who Lived: Using Harry Potter and other Fictional Characters to Help Grieving Children and Adolescents.* Abingdon: Routledge.

Melvin, D. and Lukeman, D. (2000) 'Bereavement: A framework for those working with children.' *Clinical Child Psychology and Psychiatry 5*, 4, 521–539.

Mitchell, A.J. (2010) 'Screening Procedures for Psychosocial Distress.' In J.C. Holland, W.S. Breitbar, P.B. Jacobsen, M.S. Lederberg, M.J. Loscalzo and R. McCorkle (eds) *Psych-Oncology.* Oxford: Oxford University Press.

Moore, C.W., Pengelly, M. and Rauch P.K. (2010) 'Communicating with Children when a Parent Is Dying.' In D.W. Kissane, B.D. Bultz, P.M. Butow and I.G. Finlay (eds) *Handbook of Communication in Oncology and Palliative Care.* Oxford: Oxford University Press.

Motor Neurone Disease Association (2009) *When Someone Close Has MND: A Workbook for Children aged Four to Ten.* Northampton: Motor Neurone Disease Association.

Quinton, D. (2006) 'Self-development.' In J. Aldgate, D. Jones, W. Rose and C. Jeffery (eds) *The Developing World of the Child.* London: Jessica Kingsley Publishers.

Randall, F. and Downie, R.S. (2005) *Palliative Care Ethics: A Companion for all Specialties.* Oxford: Oxford University Press.

Rauch, P.K., Muriel, A.C. and Cassem, N.H. (2002) 'Parents with cancer: Who's looking after the children?' *Journal of Clinical Oncology 20*, 21, 4399–4402.

Reith, M. and Payne, M. (2009) *Social Work in End-of-Life and Palliative Care.* Bristol: Policy Press.

Ribbens McCarthy, J. (2007) '"They all look as if they're coping, but I'm not": The relational power/lessness of "youth" in responding to experiences of bereavement.' *Journal of Youth Studies 10*, 3, 285–303.

Riches, G. and Dawson, P. (2000) *An Intimate Loneliness: Supporting Bereaved Parents and Siblings.* Buckingham: Open University Press.

Rosenblatt, P.C. (2000) *Parent Grief: Narratives of Loss and Relationship.* Philadelphia, PA: Taylor & Francis Group.

Rowling, L. (2003) *Grief in School Communities: Effective Support Strategies.* Buckingham: Open University Press.

Saldinger, A., Porterfield, K. and Cain, A.C. (2004a) 'Meeting the needs of parentally bereaved children: A framework for child-centred parenting.' *Psychiatry 67*, 4, 331–352.

Saldinger, A., Cain, A.C., Porterfield, K. and Lohnes, K. (2004b) 'Facilitating attachment between school-aged children and a dying parent.' *Death Studies 28*, 10, 915–940.

Seden, J. (2006) 'Frameworks and Theories.' In J. Aldgate, D. Jones, W. Rose and C. Jeffery (eds) *The Developing World of the Child.* London: Jessica Kingsley Publishers.

Siegel, K., Mesagno, F.P. and Christ, G. (1990) 'A prevention program for bereaved children.' *American Journal of Orthopsychiatry 60*, 2, 168–175.

Silverman, P.R. (2000) *Never too Young to Know: Death in Children's Lives.* Oxford: Oxford University Press.

Smaje, C. and Field, D. (1997) 'Absent Minorities? Ethnicity and the Use of Palliative Care Services.' In D. Field, J. Hockey and N. Small (eds) *Death, Gender and Ethnicity.* London: Routledge.

Smith, S.C. (1999) *The Forgotten Mourners* (2nd edition). London: Jessica Kingsley Publishers.

Stokes, J. (2004) *Then, Now and Always: Supporting Children as They Journey through Grief – A Practitioner's Guide.* Cheltenham: Winston's Wish.

Stokes, J.A. and Bailey, P. (2000) *The Secret C: Straight Talking about Cancer.* Cheltenham: Winston's Wish.

Stroebe, M. and Schut, H.A.W. (1999) 'The dual process model of coping with bereavement: Rationale and description.' *Death Studies 23*, 3, 197–224.

Thastum, M., Johansen, M.B., Gubba, L., Olesen, L.B. and Romer, G. (2008) 'Coping, social relations, and communication: A qualitative exploratory study of children of parents with cancer.' *Clinical Child Psychology and Psychiatry 13*, 1, 123–138.

The, A.M. (2002) *Palliative Care and Communication: Experiences in the Clinic.* Buckingham: Open University Press.

Thomas, K. (2011) 'Overview and Introduction to Advance Care Planning.' In K. Thomas (ed.) *Advance Care Planning in End of Life Care.* Oxford: Oxford University Press.

Turner, J., Kelly, B., Swanson, C., Allison, R. and Wetzig, N. (2005) 'Psychosocial impact of newly diagnosed advanced breast cancer.' *Psycho-Oncology 14*, 5, 396–407.

United Nations (1989) *UN Convention on the Rights of the Child.* Available at www.unicef.org.uk/UNICEFs-Work/Our-mission/UN-Convention, accessed on 30 October 2011.

Vint, P.E. (2005a) 'An exploration of the support available to children who may wish to visit a critically adult in ITU.' *Intensive and Critical Care Nursing 21*, 3, 149–159.

Vint, P.E. (2005b) 'Children visiting adults in ITU – what support is available? A descriptive study.' *Nursing in Critical Care 10*, 2, 64–71.

Walter, T. (1991) 'Modern death: Taboo or not taboo?' *Sociology 25*, 2, 293–310.

Waskett, D.A. (1995) 'Chairing the Child – A Seat of Bereavement.' In S.C. Smith and M. Pennells (eds) *Interventions with Bereaved Children.* London: Jessica Kingsley Publishers.

Way, P. (2009) 'Bereavement, Children and Families.' In Y. Gunaratnam and D. Oliviere (eds) *Narrative and Stories in Health Care: Illness, Dying, and Bereavement.* Oxford: Oxford University Press.

Weber, Z., Rowling, L. and Scanlon, L. (2007) '"It's like…a confronting issue": Life-changing narratives of young people.' *Qualitative Health Research 17*, 7, 945–953.

Welch, A.S., Wadsworth, M.E. and Compas, B.E. (1996) 'Adjustment of children and adolescents to parental cancer: Parents' and children's perspectives.' *Cancer 77*, 7, 1409–1418.

Willis, S. (2005) 'Work with Bereaved Children.' In B. Monroe and F. Kraus (eds) *Brief Interventions with Bereaved Children.* Oxford: Oxford University Press.

Wright, B. (1991) *Sudden Death: A Research Base for Practice.* Edinburgh: Churchill Livingstone.

Index

29786351R00111

Printed in Great
Britain
by Amazon